The
Body Language
of Sex, Power, and
Aggression

JULIUS FAST

The Body Language

of Sex, Power, and Aggression

M. EVANS AND COMPANY, INC. New York, N.Y. 10017

M. Evans and Company titles are distributed in
the United States by the J. B. Lippincott Company,
East Washington Square, Philadelphia, Pa. 19105;
and in Canada by McClelland & Stewart Ltd.,
25 Hollinger Road, Toronto M4B 3G2, Ontario

LIBRARY OF CONGRESS CATALOGING IN PUBLICATION DATA

Fast, Julius, 1918-
    The body language of sex, power, and aggression.

    1. Nonverbal communication (Psychology)   2. Sex
(Psychology)   3. Control (Psychology)   4. Aggressiveness
(Psychology)   I. Title.
BF637.C45F37   152.3'84   76-47665
ISBN 0-87131-220-0

Design by Joel Schick

Manufactured in the United States of America

9 8 7 6 5 4 3 2 1

Contents

Foreword

When I finished the last correction on the galleys of
Body Language, some six years ago, and it was safely off
to the printers, I thought I was done with it and I could
turn all my attention to another project. I was completely
wrong. In terms of the amount of time I've spent on the
subject since then, I was just begnning to become ac-
quainted with body language.

In the years since the book's publication, I have been
on dozens of television shows and have lectured to groups
all over the United States, groups ranging from teachers'

organizations to trial lawyers and including industrial relations outfits, colleges, medical societies, women's clubs
and business men.

I have been involved in encounter groups and sensitivity sessions, have taught a class on the subject and have
been called in as a consultant to politicians and indus-
trialists.

I have, in short, been completely overwhelmed by what
seemed to me, at the very beginning, a very obvious fact
—we communicate with our bodies as well as with our
words. When I taught body language I told my students,
"I'm not going to teach you something new or original.
I'm simply going to open your eyes to what you already
know, to a language all of you use fluently."

Body language is just that, a language we all use and
understand. But it is an unconscious language, and because of that it is a very honest language. While you can
easily lie with words, it is a lot harder to lie with your
body. The classic proof of this occurred on television
some years back, and the entire nation saw it.

Former President Nixon held a press conference to reassure the nation that our incursion into Cambodia was
temporary and would not escalate the war. His voice was
smooth, his body movement projected sincerity, and the
over-all impression was confidence. Then one newsman
began asking some pointed and probing questions about
how long we intended to stay in Cambodia.

Again the President reacted smoothly, but an alert TV
cameraman cut in for a tight shot of the President's fist,

clasped so rigidly that the knuckles were white. He held that shot for the entire answer, and that one, tense body-language gesture projected rigidity and broadcast a complete contradiction to everything the President was saying.

Knowing how important body language is to politicians who wish to project an air of sincerity, I am not surprised at the flood of questions I have had from them. Nor am I surprised at the hundreds of questions I have had from lawyers' associations over the years. They too have a need to know how they can master this newly discovered, but old, old language.

How old is body language? It probably arose long before humans learned to speak. Certainly men have been aware of it for thousands of years. On a television talk show, Hugh Downs pointed out to me that during the first century A.D. Marcus Fabius Quintilianus, a Roman rhetorician, held that body language gestures could add to the dramatic impact of orations.

What did surprise me, wherever I talked, were the hundreds of people—students, parents, children, husbands, wives—who pressed me for answers to very personal questions—who saw, in body language, a means of getting a little closer to each other, of gaining some meaningful insights, of communicating on a deeper, more honest level, of solving their own family problems.

There was the housewife in a TV audience in Cleveland who, during a question period, fixed me with a searching stare and asked, "Why does my husband tell

me that I don't know how to look at people?" As she
talked, her eye contact was so intense and beseaching
that I could hardly bear it.

And of course there were many who saw body language as a "fun and games" thing, a way of broadening
their pleasure potential. One of my students, a handsome
young New Yorker, was quite frank about his reason
for taking the course. "I'm into the singles bar scene, and
I want to learn more about picking up girls."

At the end of the course, I asked him if he had gotten
what he was after. "It's wild," he told me. "I realize that
I used to come on wrong, turn the girls off with the
wrong signals. Now I've changed. I walk into a bar and
I know exactly who to talk to, who's going to respond,
how to let her know I dig her."

There was a young bearded lawyer in Colorado who
asked me, "Do you think my beard projects the wrong
image in court?"

I couldn't answer that except to say, "It depends on the
judge, on the image you want to project in court, on the
case you're involved in and on your age. Does the beard
say *wisdom,* or does it say *hippy?* Does it go with a suit
and tie and neat hair and say, *Member of the establish-
ment, but not into a rigid pattern,* or does it go with jeans
and an open shirt and beads and say, *a bit of a rebel who
goes against convention?*"

As with any body language gesture, a beard is only one
part of the total man.

Whatever the questioners' motives were, they all

needed answers, and very soon I became involved in research again, checking out those centers across the nation where body language was being studied and analyzed by psychologists, choreographers, dramatic coaches and image makers. I was invited to join a public relations firm setting up a non-verbal communication department for the election year, a team of clinical psychologists who wanted to open up a center for body language in therapy, and on and on. I declined all for reasons of time, morality, and lack of scientific training, but I picked brains mercilessly and kept notes and files.

As my files grew, and as the letters poured in with new questions, I began to realize that in spite of the many repeats the pattern of questioning ran in only three directions. People were curious about sex, power and aggression.

This book is the result of those letters and that research. I've defined each of the three areas broadly and inevitably there had to be some overlap, but I think that almost every question on body language has been posed and answered—but I thought that when *Body Language* itself was first published.

—*Julius Fast*

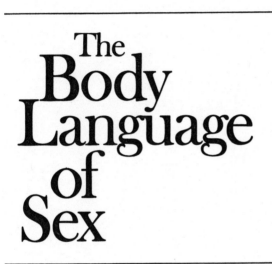

The
Body
Language
of
Sex

My husband and I are in our late fifties, and, while we've always had a good sex life, recently my husband seems less interested in sex—which I suppose is very natural at our age. But at the same time he wants me to touch him more, to stimulate him more. What does this mean?

I would think his desire to be stimulated by more touch is a sign of his continuing interest in you. Your husband still wants the sexual relations you've both enjoyed during your marriage.

Dr. Harold Lief, director of the Marriage Council of Philadelphia, has written that with age a man is less easily aroused sexually through the cortex, but he needs greater stimulation locally. In other words, the body contact your husband asks for now is the physical trigger that will release his love for you.

My girlfriend says women are equal to men in every way, but obviously their bodies are different. Is their body language different, too?

It is very different. Over and above the differences that are physical, there are the ones that are culturally acquired, the ones we learn as children. Girl babies are handled more gently and delicately by their parents, and, as they grow, are told that certain movements (such as sitting with their knees apart or taking large strides) are too unladylike, too boisterous. Boys are encouraged to be manly—to move with a sure, assertive purposefulness— and any rough activity they engage in is shrugged off, since "boys will be boys."

A woman friend of mine who enjoys jogging and other athletic pursuits was striding down the street enjoying the spring air, when a man passing by said, "Looks like one of those typical libbers." This is a good example of a kind of totally artificial distinction between men and women made real by cultural conditioning.

Another example of a culturally conditioned sex difference shows in the way most women throw a baseball. Part of the reason most women can't throw as far as men is that they've been conditioned to feel that moving the arm from the elbow to the shoulder too far away from the body is an unladylike gesture—so they tend to throw from the wrist and lower arm. (And how often do you see women sitting with their hands clasped behind their head? That, too, involves moving the upper arm away from the body, and so, to many women, feels "unfeminine.")

Still another example of a culturally determined body language is the way in which homosexuals of either sex tend to parody the body language of the other sex. But one thing always missing from the impersonations is the unconscious use of gender signals.

I've heard the term gender signal used before, but I've never understood what it means. For that matter, what are the gender signals?

Very simply, gender signals are masculine and feminine body movements. As an example, most American men cross their legs with their knees open. When a woman in the United States walks, her pelvis tips forward and up, her arms are held close to her body, and they usually swing from the elbows down.

When men walk, they keep their thighs apart, roll their pelvis back, and swing their arms from the shoulders.

Women tend to close their eyes more slowly than men. The quick blink is considered a masculine signal.

The way we hold our hands at the wrist is related to gender. The limp-wristed gesture is feminine—at least in the United States.

Showing the palm of the hand is also a feminine gesture, usually associated with courting. But like any courting gesture, showing the palm can also be used when sex is not involved. Qualifiers turn off the sexual implication and leave only the "I want to be friends" impact.

The qualifiers that turn off a courting gender signal, that modify or contradict it, can be gestures as simple as twisting a wedding ring. Or the context of the courting gesture can alter its meaning. Watch any woman in politics as she gives a speech; chances are you'll see her show her palms to "court" the audience in body language.

What are some other courting gender signals?

The most obvious gesture for a woman is the lifted hand that pushes back the hair from the face or rearranges it above the ears. It's a flirtatious gesture, and it spells femininity.

The equivalent in the man is the unconscious adjustment of the tie. Watch a man who has just been introduced to an attractive woman. Within the first five minutes, you can often count three or four preening gestures (another name for courting gestures): touching the tie or the jacket lapels, straightening the creases in the pants.

Touching the lips with the tongue is often a courting gesture for women, and their eyes come into play fairly often with long looks and side glances. Another courting gesture common to both men and women is to fondle something—a glass, a keychain, an ashtray—or to "caress" your own body.

Often courting signals are unconscious, and it's only the knowledgeable third-party observer who can understand what is going on. In this stylized, unconscious courting, women may reveal their thighs by crossing their legs, or if they're standing, put one hand on their hip and tilt their body.

But while most often these gestures are used to signify an interest in the other sex, in many cases the same gesture may be used to discharge anxiety. We must always examine the context of the gesture.

Our little baby is only a few months old, but she acts like a regular flirt with my husband. He claims her gestures and flirting are inherently "female." Could this be so? At what age do boys and girls begin to use different body language?

We haven't yet discovered the exact age that separates the boys from the girls—in body language. Many babies, like yours, seem to use feminine or masculine body language not long after birth.

But we do know that by four or five years of age, children are definitely using the body language associated with their own sex. When my daughter was about five, she tended to take much smaller steps than my son did when he was that age. And I remember that even when my son was young, he'd always look me straight in the eye when I yelled at him, while my daughter would lower her eyes at the first sign that I was angry. We encourage male children to be more assertive, and their body language is, consequently, more assertive than that of female children.

By the time children reach adolescence, a whole new lexicon has been added to their body language vocabulary. A teen-age girl with her developing breasts learns to carry them provocatively or to hunch forward shyly in an attempt to hide them. The boy, too, learns how to move his developing body in a masculine manner. He learns to be comfortable with his new height, learns to hold his shoulders back to show off their breadth. By the time they have passed through to adulthood, both sexes have usually accepted and grown into their own special body language.

I am in my early sixties and my husband is five years older. We've been married for thirty-five years, and it's been a very good marriage in all ways, but lately we've

had a very unhappy sexual problem. My husband has been impotent. Since it happened, I've noticed that he's been reluctant to touch me. Now I avoid touching him bcause I'm afraid to upset him. We used to be very loving, hugging and kissing each other even when sex was not involved. How can I get back to that loving state without threatening my husband?

Many men, as they grow older, experience periods of impotence. If these are treated as no more than a temporary obstacle to sex, they will usually resolve themselves, and the ability to have sex will return. But often the impotence becomes a psychological block to any further sex. Because he is afraid of failure, the man stops trying, and this seems to be what has happened to your husband.

Dr. Harold Lief, director of the Marriage Council of Philadelphia, cites a very similar case in which a couple, refraining from any physical contact because they feared it would arouse sexual desires that could not be satisfied, were told that touching and hugging in themselves could be satisfying and acceptable expressions of love.

They were taught how to exchange affection without the demands of sex, and they were startled to discover how much they enjoyed the touching and caressing, the tactile expressions of love.

In discussing what happened, Dr. Lief said, "The strange thing is that when they started to do this, back came the husband's capacity for erection!"

In the great majority of cases, Dr. Lief stresses, the impotence of age is psychological. The treatment is usually to stop the demand for sexual performance and let the couple rediscover their bodies while they communicate with each other through body language—without anxiety.

Whenever my girlfriend and I have sex, I end up with a back full of scratches, and a few very obvious bites around the shoulders. Is biting and scratching a normal part of the body language of sex? What does it mean?

No one can set any standards for what is and isn't normal in sexual relations. The only guideline most people agree on is that anything is acceptable if you and your partner both enjoy it and it hurts neither of you—nor anyone else.

Scratching can be a sign of the intensity of your lovemaking or the expression of a sadistic impulse. But almost all men respond to being scratched by their sexual partner and interpret it positively. To them it's a signal that they're turning a woman on, that they are doing all the right things. Many women are very negative about being scratched during sex, but a few welcome it as a sign of healthy masculine aggression. It turns them on, too.

Like all body language messages, this tactile one may mean many things, but most people see it as a positive—and powerful—release of sexual energy.

My wife always talks me into taking the kids along when we go for a walk. I feel that they cramp our style, but she claims they help us communicate even if we don't speak. How could this be? Can children affect body language?

They can, but not in the way your wife thinks. A team of seven researchers at the University of Minnesota went out during the summer of 1972 and observed 440 couples with and without children at shopping malls, in business districts, at the zoo, outside churches and at the beach. They watched very closely and without being noticed to see whether each person in the couple was touching, smiling at, or talking to the other.

The Minnesota researchers found that when men and women were with children they touched each other less, talked to each other less, and smiled at each other less. Children just seemed to get in the way of any kind of communication!

These results would seem to prove your wife wrong. It might be a better idea to leave the kids at home when you go out together—or at least to try and increase the time you are alone.

The researchers admit that most older people who have been together for a long time tend to talk less and touch less anyway. Familiarity, if it doesn't breed contempt, at least seems to breed disinterest. But even taking this factor into account, the researchers assure us that children inhibit communication.

As for smiling, they admit that adults who are alone have more to smile about because they're usually interested in each other. "Young adults of courting age," they point out, at dances, on the beach, may smile a great deal and make us think that if children were around they'd smile less. The truth is, it's the "country, the beach, the dances that increase smiling."

All is not hopeless, however. Lest anyone should avoid having children for fear they would cut down on his smiling, talking, and touching, the Minnesota team notes that though children may be a source of difficulty to their parents, they still increase the ties between the parents. They still offer substantial rewards to the parents, and even if the parents touch, smile, and talk less when the kids are around, they may enjoy the touching, talking, and smiling more.

I've been dating a girl for three weeks, and I feel like I'm getting ambivalent signals from her. Are there any body language signals that will tell me for sure how she really feels about me?

There are, of course, all the obvious body language signals. Does she smile when you're around? Does she look toward you often if you're separated at a party? Does she seem relaxed when she's alone with you—or does her body posture become stiff and uncomfortable?

Does she touch you, hold your hand, want to be close to you physically?

Most people take note of all these signals unconsciously and resolve them in their unconscious mind. Their conscious mind then becomes aware of the answer: She/he likes me, or doesn't like me.

As a rule, you won't choose someone for a girlfriend unless your subconscious has already added up all the body language signals and made a decision. We call that decision *attraction* or *chemistry* or *interest*. In actuality, it's a mental computer process.

There is also a very subtle clue to like and dislike. Scientists investigating "pupillometrics" report that when you see a person you like, the pupils of your eyes respond by growing larger. Watch for this the next time your girlfriend sees you.

I met a wonderful girl at a party about a month ago, and we've been going around together ever since. The only problem is, she doesn't seem to realize that I'm interested in her sexually. How can I use body language to let her know that I want to go bed with her? I'm just too inhibited to blurt it out!

Your way of looking at her is the chief body language signal here. Glancing at her body and letting her see the glance is considered, by both men and women, a provocative and seductive act.

In body contact, you must go beyond mere touching and let your touch become a caress.

According to questionnaire studies among college students, some of the body language gestures that spell out desire are wetting the lips, passing the tip of the tongue over the lips, and—oddly enough—in married people, playing with the wedding ring. This seems strange because the same gesture, used when a man and woman are talking to each other on nonintimate terms, says "I'm married and safe!" But, as with any body language gesture, the total context of the situation is what counts. If you are a married man and your intention of seducing the woman is getting across, the wedding ring gesture sort of spells it all out.

The most obvious signal for wanting further sexual relations is the deep kind of kissing that leads to sexual intimacy. But this presumes that you have built up all the steps in between.

As an interesting sidelight on what kissing can signal, in England during World War II the English girls and the American GIs ran into a body language impasse. The girls considered the Americans too fast while the GIs thought the English girls were too fast.

Some careful research on the part of an army psychologist uncovered the fact that in England, at that time, it was considered customary for a girl to go to bed with a man shortly after he had kissed her. It usually took a long time before that first kiss was given.

Americans, on the other hand, were used to kissing at the start of a friendship, and then expected a long time before getting the girl into bed. The English girls, the Americans thought, were fast because it was kiss and into the sack. The girls thought the soldiers fast because they wanted to kiss right away—and by English standards, this meant going to bed right away, too!

I've been having an affair with a man I love very deeply, but he always wants to begin intercourse too soon, while I still want more foreplay. How can I let him know what I want?

You can tell your partner a tremendous amount by the movement of your body. You can change position by moving gently away, or you can subtly push his body to the position you want. In all of this, your movements should be gentle and ever playful.

Masters and Johnson, in their study of human sexuality, suggest that since each partner knows his or her own body and its needs, they should guide each other into those ways that pleasure them best.

The most important thing in using body language to communicate your needs during the act of love is to avoid giving your partner any feeling that you're rejecting him or withdrawing from the situation. One way to be sure of this is to initiate some different types of foreplay your-self without giving your partner the sense that he's in-experienced.

I was at a friend's house recently when I met this really far-out girl. I could tell she was turned on to me because she moved closer to me on the couch, but her date was sitting on her other side. Was there any way I could have let her know I liked her without annoying her date? He's a football player!

The smile is always a useful signal to let her know just how much her appearance pleases you. Since she took the first step by moving closer, you could have responded and moved toward her. It shows that you not only recog-nize her signal, but you're also answering it with a posi-tive signal of your own.

An *accidental* touch or a brush against her is a further signal of your interest. You might touch her arm or thigh—or even let your foot touch hers without her date knowing it. A lovely turn-of-the-century drawing by Charles Dana Gibson shows a man and woman, under the girl's mama's watchful eye, making body contact un-der the table with their feet while both look innocent and demure. If body contact is established, don't move away.

Of course, catching her eye and holding it speaks volumes, but don't let her date catch you at it. You're right to be careful with football players!

I have a boyfriend I like very much, but he drives me up a wall when I speak to him. Sometimes he's just fine, but there are other times when I get confused. I interrupt him while he's still speaking, or I wait for him to continue when he's finished. Often there'll be long pauses before he answers me, and I feel as if I've lost him. What's going on?

In conversation, we signal each other with many small gestures called markers. These tell us when someone is finished talking and when the other should start. In this way, a conversation proceeds normally. Your friend's perception of body language signals and markers seems to be out of synch.

When we ask a question, for example, our head lifts at the end of the sentence, or we may raise our hand or the pitch of our voice. If we want to signal that we intend to keep on talking, we keep our head, hand, or voice level. When we answer a question, we lower our head at the end of the answer.

If we forget these signals, or deliberately don't use them, or don't know how to use them, the conversation is often awkward. When one partner takes too long to respond, ignoring our signal to start, we may interpret his hesitance as withdrawal or rejection. This may be what is happening between you and your friend. Take a good look at his head and hand movements next time you talk, and try to read the body language signals he's sending you.

I know that body language is different in different cultures, but it seems to me that there must be some signals that cut across every land. When I was in France recently I was able to pick up people my own age by using the same flirting technique I had learned in the States, a sideways glance and a smile. If things are so different in different lands, why did this work so well?

First of all, while some signals are different, many are the same from culture to culture. We borrow body language from other cultures just as we borrow words. The movies are the greatest source of cross-cultural body language borrowing.

Second, your flirting signal worked in France because it is a part of French body language. The gesture you used is one compounded of eye and eyebrow movements combined with a smile. In doing it, the eyebrows are jerked upward for about one-sixth of a second—so small a time that its impact is subliminal—and the glance is given from the corner of the eye. It's a simple greeting, a look that in essence says "hello!," then slides away before it can be answered.

The accompanying smile, of course, does a great deal. It says you're interested and receptive, and it invites the man to take the initiative.

In tests in primitive tribes in various parts of the world, the smile was found to be the only universal body language signal, and the ability to smile is undoubtedly inherited. We never have to learn how to do it. We're born with the knowledge.

The greeting with the eyes, the flirting glance, is another matter. Irenaus Eibl-Eibesfeldt, a German behavioral scientist, used cameras and mirrorlike attachments that permitted him to film people all over the world without their knowledge. With each picture, he wrote down the social context in which the filmed incident occurred.

Comparing his films, he found that among the most different people in the world, Balinese, Papuans, French, and Waika Indians, a rapid raising and lowering of the eyebrows accompanied by a smile and often a nod was used as a friendly flirting gesture—the same sort of gesture you describe. It worked for you in the States and in France, too. Eibl-Eibesfeldt found that it works all over the world.

He likens this flirting glance to one of the gestures passed down from "an ancient evolutionary inheritance." Other inherited gestures, according to this German behaviorist, are rotating our arms inward and raising our shoulders when we're threatened, pulling the corners of our mouths down when we're angry, exposing upper canine teeth which are no longer large enough to be dangerous when we're annoyed, and, in women, lowering the eyelids and head as they look away. This, he feels is a evolutionary remnant of the animal's flight reaction.

These findings of hereditary signals in our body language lexicon contradict the idea that only the smile is inherited, but, as with any new science, the final word is still not in. Now genetics has the edge. Further research may give it back to environment.

I spent an entire evening last week sitting in the living room with my boyfriend and kissing—just that, kissing! We both enjoyed it so much that afterward I began to wonder *why* do people enjoy kissing so? Is it the body language in the act? And what does it say? How did it start?

Kissing is body language, of course, and it says a variety of things. There is the very perfunctory kiss where the lips hardly connect and the message is just as vague. It may be "I like you," and it may be "I'm not even fully aware of you." It's a ritualized gesture. At the other end of the scale is the deep, erotic kissing you and your boyfriend enjoyed. To some people, this type of kissing is almost as satisfying as sexual intercourse and carries the same message of delight and love and pleasuring.

In between are all the ranges of kissing—from the mother who kisses her child, to the friends who kiss when they meet, the good-bye kiss and the hello kiss, the greeting kiss in France and other foreign countries, and the Mafia kiss of death as well as the often perfunctory husband-wife kiss in the morning.

Where did kissing start and why? That's a question that still isn't completely answered, though we have some good ideas about it. In the animal world, birds seem to do a good deal of kissing, but their kissing is an offshoot of a feeding procedure. Mother birds chew up and partially digest the food, then regurgitate it to pass it on to the babies. Gorillas, chimpanzees and orangutans practice mouth-to-mouth feeding. This has been observed in zoos as well as in the wild, and not only between mother and baby, but also between adults. In fact, adult chimps in the wild, according to animal behaviorist Jane Goodall, greet each other by touching lips when they meet, without passing food.

This would indicate that the human kiss also derived from passing food, and there are still some primitive people who chew and predigest their food, then pass it by mouth to their children.

A German anthropologist, Dr. L. Hormann, writing before World War I, noted that young people in the Tyrol used to chew resin as we chew gum. In courting, a boy would offer some chewed resin to a girl. If she accepted, she would have to press her mouth to his while she bit the resin from between his teeth. The play involved a lot of fun and enforced kissing.

A search through the courting habits of other European countries will turn up a great many connections between kissing and feeding. Some European swains bring their fiancées food which must be eaten with kisses. Others pass wine from mouth to mouth.

In kissing, the same movements occur as in food passing.

There are very few human cultures that do not kiss. Darwin reported that kissing was not an innate act, and that many people did not know about it, that New Zealanders, Tahitians, and Australians do not kiss, but later research has proved him wrong. There is always kissing between mother and child, but in some cultures it becomes taboo in adult life or changes to nose rubbing.

I'm twenty-four years old, and one of my problems is getting along with people in a conversation. I'll meet a guy or a gal and get to rapping with them, and then, for some reason or other, I seem to lose them. I don't think it's because I'm any more boring than the next guy, but one girl told me I wasn't responding with the right body signals. What are the signals?

What she was probably referring to, in your case, was a lack of feedback. For example, in any conversation between two people, there is a lot of head nodding back and forth. The nodding serves a number of purposes. The most obvious is agreement. Jim and Sarah are talking; Sarah says something Jim agrees with, and he nods. Assured that she is reaching Jim, Sarah continues in the same vein. The nod on Jim's part has sent the message, "You're right. Keep talking. I want to hear more."

If Jim stops nodding, he signals that he doesn't accept what Sarah says, or that he's not really interested. Sarah, failing to get the feedback of the nod, changes the conversation—or just turns off to Jim.

Not everyone nods to the same degree, but when you speak to someone who doesn't nod or react at all, no matter what you say, then you're put off stride and eventually, if there's no body feedback of any kind, you know you're just not reaching him. In that case most people give up and lose interest in the conversation.

If this is your problem—and you can decide if it is by some careful observation of yourself and a few heart-to-heart talks with friends—then you can try to solve it by making yourself nod, from time to time, if you agree with the person who's talking. Watch how others do this to get the right rhythm and intensity. The feedback generated by your nods will encourage your partner to go on talking.

The nodding needn't be overdone to the point of making you seem like a "yes" man, but it should be done just enough to give a sense of security to the other person.

This same feedback operates in public speaking. When you address an audience, you watch for the nods of agreement; they signal that you're on the right track and you can proceed with what you're saying. Nothing is more devastating than addressing a dead audience with no feedback. To avoid this, if you feel too little feedback, too little response, search out one person who agrees with you and nods to tell you so, and make eye contact with him. The reassurance you get will help you in your delivery.

It's the acute awareness of feedback and the ability to zero in on the subject that causes it that makes a good public speaker.

I'm gay, and I live in a small town in the Midwest. I can usually meet other gay men when I go to one of the big cities. Their body language is pretty obvious. But I have a feeling there are a lot of men like me in my own hometown. Are there body language signals that gay men send out to each other that I could learn to recognize?

There are many obvious signals and many subtle ones. In a small town such as yours, very few gay men are open about their sexual life. They have had to mask their homosexuality for survival, and usually the masks are very effective.

Eye contact is a standard signal among gay men, even as it is among heterosexual men and women. For every social situation there is a *moral looking time*—the length of time it is proper to catch and hold someone else's eye. When you pass someone on the street, the moral looking time is only a second or two. If one man holds another's eye longer than that, he may be signaling a number of things. "Do I know you?" "I'm friendly and I want to say hello." "I'm sure I've seen you before."

In most of these messages, a smile and a nod confirm the meaning. When there is no smile or nod and the eye is held too long, the meaning changes. It may be "You are a stranger." "You look peculiar." Or "I am interested in you sexually."

This extralong eye contact is one of the most common signals used between two gay men. The followup signal, after they've passed each other, is to turn and look back. From there it can proceed as any heterosexual pickup does.

There are other obvious signals that allow one homosexual to recognize another. In years gone by, a red necktie sometimes served to announce the gay to anyone who recognized the signal. Obviously, not every man who wore a red tie was gay, but it was a starting point.

Today, the signals are just as obvious but less well known. A single earring or a bunch of keys clipped to the belt and worn with jeans and a leather jacket send their own body language signal to the gay world. Worn on the left, the earring or keys signal "I'm aggressive"; worn on the right they signal, "I'm passive."

Unfortunately for the gay world, the keys on the belt is not always a gay giveaway. Many heterosexual men wear keys clipped to the belt as a type of jewelry. So the gay subculture has taken to wearing a handkerchief, half tucked into the back pocket, as a signal: aggressive on the left side, passive on the right.

With the handkerchief, a color code has developed: black ones for sadists and masochists, green for bondage and discipline, mustard color for genital size, and blue for conventional sex—all with the left-right, aggressive-passive code.

The color signals have begun to spread out, according to a number of gay authorities. Colored bumper stickers are available for the gay men who want to pick up others in cars, and small colored tie tacks for the gay business-man who wants to send a message to his fellow executives.

My husband and I had some friends in to dinner last week, and after they left we got into one of our ongoing hassles. It happens every time we entertain. I feel that he doesn't respond to all the little signals people send out, and he claims I'm just imagining such signals where there aren't any. Eventually our argument boils down to who's more sensitive at reading body language, men or women. Have you an answer to that?

I have, and you win the argument. Usually women *are* more sensitive to body language. A series of tests designed to reveal a profile of nonverbal sensitivity (PONS) has been developed by a team of five psychologists at Harvard University. The person taking the tests is presented with a film of a series of scenes emphasizing facial expressions with only a few spoken phrases that are never clearly heard—it's like turning the sound off on a TV soap opera.

After viewing each scene, the person taking the test chooses a situational label from two possibilities. A typical scene will show a woman's face for a few seconds. She appears upset and she's saying something, but you can't quite understand her words.

The testee must choose between "jealous anger" or "talking about her divorce." Only one is correct. The idea is to see who does well, and who does poorly in recognizing the true message behind the nonverbal or body language signals.

According to the test, women are better at this game than men. Out of ninety-eight sample groups in which two or more men and women participated, the women scored higher in eighty-one groups.

The investigators suggest that the difference in perception between men and women becomes less, and even reverses itself—the men coming out ahead—when the men tested have occupations considered "artistic, expressive, or nurturant." Men who were actors, artists, designers, psychiatrists, clinical psychologists, college students in visual courses, and schoolteachers tended to score as high or higher than women.

This would indicate that the ability to excel at body language is—as is body language itself—hooked to the culture. The culture demands more sensitivity from women, and they live up to the demands and become more sensitive. It also demands more sensitivity from this group of men, and they too meet the demands. In the final analysis, the more sensitive you are, the better you are at reading body language.

So, in fuller answer to your question, it is not being a man or a woman that makes one a better body language reader. You gain the skill by playing the role demanded of women in this society.

I've noticed that when my boyfriend and I are having a rap session, he seems to blink much more than usual. Does this mean he doesn't agree with me?

Generally, a high frequency of blinking is supposed to indicate a very intense attention span. In other words, your boyfriend is really listening. Whether he agrees with you or not is a different story. This depends on all the other signals he sends.

This blinking to indicate attention is one body language element in communication, but you must remember that blinking is also one of the physical devices the body uses to keep itself in shape. The tissue of the eyeball is unprotected, and it can get very uncomfortable if it dries out or if dust falls on it. For this reason, our lids act as washer-wipers and lubricate the eyeballs with tears during the blink.

Those people whose eyes tend to dry out easily or whose ducts don't secrete enough tears will blink more often than others, so there are two possible reasons why your boyfriend blinks. If it occurs only when he's listening to you, he's really listening.

I'm fifteen years old, and I have this boyfriend I like very much. My problem is, I can talk to him over the phone for hours, but when we get together I always feel awkward and uncomfortable, and it's very hard to say

anything. If body language is such a big part of communication, why isn't it easier for us to talk when we see each other? I don't feel this way with my girlfriend. We can talk to each other over the phone or in person.

Body language adds a tremendous amount to communication, it's true, but a conversation over a telephone can be much safer for this very reason. While you don't see your boyfriend, he doesn't see you either, and there is less danger in the situation and less of a threat. You can say what you please without having to watch his reaction to your words or have him watch yours.

Most adolescents still aren't sure of their own body language, and unconsciously they're afraid that they may send the wrong signs with the wrong meaning—or give themselves away by revealing what they really feel.

This may be one reason why you and your boyfriend are uncomfortable talking to each other face to face but have no problems with telephone talk. Join the club of thousands of other young men and women.

Teen-agers, incidentally, are not the only ones who face this problem. Many adults are more fluent and at ease over a telephone than in a face-to-face confrontation, and again the reason is usually a feeling of awkwardness about the signals they send with their body.

I've noticed that when I argue with my boyfriend and I begin to win the argument, he will often put the fingers of his right hand to his left cheek while his thumb touches his right cheek. What is he saying to me with this gesture?

This common defensive pose closes off the mouth. It is a shield against a verbal threat, but it also blocks any wrong argument on his part. When he realizes that you are right, he may be too deep into the argument to concede and still be comfortable with his concession. This gesture may unconsciously betray his uncertainty.

The palm of the hand touching the back of the neck is an even more defensive pose. With women, this hand-to-neck gesture often becomes a hair-smoothing gesture, a flirting or preening signal, as if to say, "Well, you're right, but let's shift from an intellectual level to a man-woman plane."

Many of us perform the hand-to-neck gesture when we feel that we're in the wrong, either consciously or unconsciously.

I was walking down the street of a European city a few months ago, and I noticed a very pretty girl window shopping. I pretended to be interested in a nearby store window, and we began to send out signals to each other. Then she started to lick her lips, and for some reason this bothered me, so much that I turned and walked away. Afterward I wasn't sure about what I felt. I don't know if I was more bothered or excited by what she did. What does it mean?

In central Europe, a signal such as the one you described means sexual availability, but the gesture has different meanings in different parts of the world. Basically, it is a ritualized form of licking. The tongue is put out very quickly with a brief licking motion either in the air or to the lips.

The gesture is used often in primitive societies, sometimes with and sometimes without the sexual overtones. It may be an innocent flirting gesture or a more eplicit sexual signal. Men will use it to women and women to men.

As for the origin of lip licking, it probably is related to the social grooming we see in animals. Many animals groom by licking their partners, and sometimes the licking becomes a part of erotic foreplay. In the few primitive societies left in the world, we find a similar pattern.

The tongue licking, possibly derived from tongue grooming, has come to mean a promise of erotic pleasure. In our relatively rigid sexual setup, it offers all sorts of forbidden oral delights.

In America, the gesture is not very common in heterosexual circles, although Marilyn Monroe turned on an entire nation of men by using it, and it is still employed on the level of prostitution and readily available sex. It is less common with the average woman. When they do use it, it's often unconscious and it is a much slower licking of the lips, as if over some very tasty morsel of food rather than as a conscious sexual come-on.

Among male homosexuals, the signal is very common in pickups. It is often used by older men toward younger ones, and it suggests, among other things, the acceptance of a passive sexual role.

Your own reaction to it, a mixture of being "bothered" and "excited," probably comes from a sort of cultural shock rather than from ignorance of the signal. On a subconscious level you were aware of the sexual overtones in the gesture. You must have been both attracted and repelled by the obviousness of the invitation.

I like a girl I go to school with, but I'm too shy to tell her how much she means to me. I've heard that you can tell someone whether or not you like them with your eyes alone. Is this true, and, if it is, how can I do it?

Studies have shown that when we like someone, or are interested in someone, we tend to look at them more often. We signal our likes and dislikes with our eyes. Literature is full of expressions that confirm this. "Her eyes never left his face." "He devoured her with his eyes." "He couldn't see enough of her." And so on. These expressions all stress the fact that when you like someone you look at them as much as you can.

The opposite is often true, too. The less you like someone, the more you avoid looking at them. "I couldn't bear to look at her. I couldn't meet his eyes."

Of course, anyone can learn to fake this very simple signal and give the impression of caring for someone who doesn't matter. We all know people who can literally hang on our every word, staring at us as we talk. If they do it skillfully, they signal "I really like you!"

If a long, steady stare bothers the other person, then the looking can be done for several short periods of time, breaking eye contact between each. The total effect is very different from the rude, prolonged stare a curious stranger sometimes gives you.

One of the girls in our crowd really knows how to flirt— without even saying a word. I've been trying to figure out how she does it, and I've discovered that she moves her eyes a lot when she blinks. What exactly does that signal to the guys?

Women do move their eyes while they blink—or to use the old-fashioned term, they "bat" their eyes. Men, on the other hand, tend to look straight ahead while blinking.

According to Dr. Henry Brosin of Pittsburgh, Pennsylvania, a former president of the American Psychiatric Association, our society interprets this blinking and eye moving as seductive. Dr. Brosin says it's all very well for a woman to do it, but it isn't socially acceptable for a man.

Dr. Brosin also notes that studies show that women

from the South are much more apt to flirt with their eyes in this manner than their northern sisters. "It's a fine-art form below the Mason-Dixon line," he says. Could your friend be a southern belle?

Sometimes, when I walk into a room at a party, I'll see a girl who looks interesting, and for some reason or other a conversation starts right away. At other times, there's just an awkward silence, and I get the feeling that she doesn't want to talk at all. But how can I sense this? Is it her body language?

Obviously, some nonverbal signaling is at work in this situation. Your experience is not unusual, and some psychologists have set out to discover just what signals are sent out in this kind of interaction. Dr. Mark Cary of the University of Pennsylvania set up a simulated situation just like the one you describe. He prepared a room with a woman sitting in it and set up a hidden television camera to observe what went on.

He asked fifteen male college students to enter the room, one at a time, and he recorded each meeting with video-tape to see when and why conversation took place.

In almost all cases, he found that the girl and the student looked at each other once as the student entered the room, but no conversation took place until the woman looked a second time.

He could not determine why the woman had control

but decided it was either her sex or the fact that she was there first and had established territorial rights.

He set up twenty situations in which a male student was in the room and a woman entered. The results were the same. It was the woman in all cases who dictated, with body language, whether or not conversation should take place. The reason? The very fact that she was a woman.

However, Cary added that the person in the room first has some control. If it's a woman who's there first, she has enormous control. If it's a man, he has some control, but this is canceled out by the fact that the entering person is a woman. Either one can initiate conversation.

In bars, Cary found a similar signaling system, but often that first, sizing-up look is omitted. The woman will only give a glance at someone who appears interesting. The glance is interpreted as permission to start a conversation.

What it boils down to is that the woman is in control of this type of pickup. If she doesn't look at all, most men will not try to talk to her.

"Inexperienced men," Cary suggests, "occasionally pick the prettiest girls to approach. More experienced men look for the girl who signals her interest in them. Because of this their score is much better."

I'm very much in love with Al, but I find that he has this one habit that bugs me. When we have sex, Al

reaches for a cigarette immediately afterward. I
haven't said anything about it to him yet, but I'm
beginning to simmer. What does it mean?

Reaching for a cigarette after sex is a very common reaction. As a nonsmoker, you may feel that Al's need for a
cigarette means he's turned off or dissatisfied. You may
begin to wonder what's wrong with the way you make
love, since you feel as if he's reaching for something more
relaxing and satisfying than sex with you.

But for a smoker, the act of reaching for a cigarette may
be an expression of satisfaction and relaxation—simply a
sign that sex was good.

I'm very much in love with a girl I want to marry, but
there's something about her sexual response that bothers
me. She claims she enjoys making love as much as I do,
but she always lies motionless during sex. There's
just no body language communication, and I wonder
if that in itself is telling me something.

You would be the person most likely to know what her
lack of movement communicates. To most men, a motionless bed partner signals that the woman is not enjoying
sex, and this signal often turns them off as well. But
lack of movement can be a confusing signal, because a
woman may be motionless during sex and still enjoy it.
She may get a tremendous enjoyment out of being domi-
nated by an aggressive man.

It is also possible that she is the victim of all those years when morality insisted that decent women do not really enjoy sex, they endure it to make their husbands happy, but they don't like it.

If this is the case, then not moving during intercourse says, in body language, "I'm not really taking part in all this. I'm doing something that's a duty, not a pleasure." Or "This is all happening in spite of myself!" Once these statements have been made to her unconscious mind, the woman can relax and enjoy it all. But it's important for you to understand—if this is the case—that this is not an intellectual decision. It happens on an emotional level.

Fortunately, few women still operate under the "sex is wrong but must be endured" doctrine.

As for you and your girlfriend, this is probably the point where body language—nonverbal communication—should be abandoned and verbal communication should take over. Talk the whole thing out!

Bill and I have only been married a year, but the two of us just aren't able to talk about sex. It's not that we're shy with each other physically—it's just difficult for us to discuss what we do. Still, I enjoy sex with Bill so much that I'd like him to know it. Is there some way I can tell him this in body language? How can I signal that I enjoy the way he makes love, or that I want intercourse again?

A smile is a time-tested method of communication. Your own look of happiness is going to tell Bill how good it's been. You can hug him closely, sigh with pleasure, and let out any sounds of enjoyment that come naturally.

To most people, it's a terrific turn-on when their sex partner cries out, groans, or sighs during the sexual act. Even without words, the vocal message indicates enjoyment beyond control.

Best of all, if you feel the enjoyment of sex with your body, let that feeling communicate itself; return his love by caressing him.

I think you are worrying needlessly. If you genuinely enjoy Bill's lovemaking, your body will—without your telling it—convey a message of satisfaction and love to your husband in a hundred different ways. What you seem to be going through is the delighted discovery many young wives make that sex can be one of the most exciting and delightful parts of marriage. This realization always seems to come as a shock if sex before marriage has been disappointing or nonexistent.

As for wanting intercourse again, the simplest signal is for you to initiate foreplay yourself. Start making love to Bill again when you're ready for it.

I am nineteen years old and I have this awful problem. I seem to always turn men on, no matter what I do. Even when I get mad at a guy and try to show him how

angry I am, unless I tell him outright he usually thinks
I'm kidding and that I really want him to make love
to me! What do you think is wrong? Is my body
language unclear?

It could be. Many people have trouble projecting a definite emotion. A study was conducted at the University of
Utah in Salt Lake City to try to discover how often this
confusion of sent and received messages takes place.

Several men and women were asked to act out six
different moods in front of a television camera. The moods
were anger, fear, seductiveness, indifference, happiness
and sadness. Then the tapes were played back for each
person, and each was asked if he were sure this was how
he meant to portray each mood. In other words, each
person checked his own performance to make sure it was
emotionally authentic.

Then the videotapes were shown to larger audiences
who were asked to identify each emotion. This, the in-
vestigaters hoped, would tell them how accurately each
man and woman signaled emotion in body language.

To their surprise, they found that most people were
only able to project two out of six moods accurately, and
those two varied from person to person. One young lady
could only project one mood, anger, and every emotion
she tried to act out was interpreted as anger. Another—
and this will be of interest to you—could only send
seductiveness. Even when she wanted to be angry, men
whistled at her.

The Utah researchers concluded that everyone sends out some misinformation on a body language level. In most cases there is a big gap between our expressions and our emotions. We say we want someone to like us, but unconsciously we send out contradictory messages with our body, our face, and our tone of voice. Our body language says "I don't like you."

Since our unconscious body language communication is often more honest than our words, we may really be saying two things at the same time—acceptance and rejection. Why? Well, we would have to be able to take a long, careful look at your inner motivation before we could answer. You send out a seductive message with your body and then deny it verbally, but perhaps the true message you want to send is the seductive one. You must look into yourself, and your motivations, a bit more carefully.

Annie is one hell of a girl and, when we're out with a bunch of friends, she's a real turn-on. But whenever I get Annie alone in my apartment, she sits on the sofa with her arms folded across her chest. What is she trying to tell me?

Crossed arms are probably the best-known body language signal. They form a protective barrier, and, depending on the rigidity of the rest of the body, they say "I'm uptight" and "It's going to take an awful lot to loosen me up."

Annie seems to be telling you that she is nervous and

anxious. Maybe her turn-on act in company is just that, an act, and once she's alone the real Annie surfaces. Or— what may be a lot worse for you—Annie may be bored with you alone.

Your best bet, if you really like Annie and you want to get her into a relaxed state, is to be gentle in your approach, and with your own body language show an open, relaxed attitude. Keep your arms open and your body loose when you sit near her on the couch, or cross your legs toward her and form half of an intimate circle that includes her. If she likes you and can relax, she may unconsciously form the other half.

Crossed arms, of course, do not always mean resistance. Sometimes they're a comfortable way to sit. But you stressed the fact that Annie only sits this way in your apartment.

You must decide yourself whether it's because Annie likes you too much that she becomes awkward with you once you're alone, or whether she likes you so little that she becomes tense. In either case, your approach should be slow, easy and relaxed. If Annie is so much fun with others, she's surely worth a lot of time and patience.

My girl and I get along beautifully. We both like the same things, and we have fun together. Sex is great, too, but we have this one crazy problem. After she's reached a climax, she wants me to hold her. I don't understand

this, because the sexual climax leaves me satiated. I want to lean back and relax or turn over and go to sleep. Does the fact that she wants to stay in my arms mean that she isn't satisfied with my lovemaking?

Satisfaction exists on many levels. A person may be satisfied sexually and still want the body language message that hugging and holding sends. Most women interpret holding after sexual intercourse as a message that there is more than physical satisfaction involved and their lover is not just using them as a sexual release.

Some men also interpret hugging after the act of sex as a statement of greater involvement, and their reluctance to do it may spring less from satiation than from a fear of getting too close or of committing themselves to a relationship they're not completely sure of. You have to examine your own motives closely to sort this out.

But there are some men and women who genuinely feel no desire for physical contact after sex—indeed, they may be troubled by it. Sometimes this reflects a problem with taking and giving love, but often it is no more than a physical preference. If the latter is the case with you, then you must use other methods to show your girlfriend that you are involved with her on more than a sexual level—if this is so.

When I was in high school, I used to wonder about the different ways that boys and girls carried their school

books. Girls almost always clasped the books to their
breasts with one or two arms while boys tended to carry
their books at their side. They'd swing them in their
fingers or cradle them by the arm or forearm. Why is this?

Part of the answer lies in the physiological differences
between men and women. Girls, once they begin to
mature, have larger hips and they are not comfortable
carrying anything at fingertip length at their side. Also,
the way the joints in a woman's arm operate make it
easier for her to carry a weight against her body, just as
the books are carried against the breast. In nature's wise
design of things, this may have been done to make it
more comfortable for a woman to carry a baby against the
breast.

There may also be a psychological shielding operation
in the young girls. The books can be a protection for the
body, shielding the developing breasts.

Boys are usually more active than girls, and the balanc-
ing that comes from extended arms is more natural to
them. Carrying books in the hands, dangling at their
sides, feels proper.

I was at a social evening a while back, and I was
sitting on the couch with a woman I like very much. We
were really into a heavy discussion when a friend came
over and said, "You two are a perfect loving circle."

He wouldn't tell us what he meant, but the phrase stuck with me. What does it mean?

When two people are in love, or extremely sympathetic to each other, you can often see a "loving circle" in the way they sit together. If they're on a couch next to each other, their bodies will be turned toward each other, their arms may meet along the back of the couch, and they'll cross their legs toward one another—in short, they'll form a circle with their bodies.

The same sort of circle, perhaps less obvious, is often formed by two people less interested in each other sexually, but still involved. The two people needn't be of different sexes. Two men and two women can also form loving circles depending on how much they enjoy each other's company or how interested each is in what the other is saying at the moment.

A year ago Charlie and I joined a young-married-couples group at our church. Many of them, like ourselves, were newlyweds. After spending an evening at the first meeting, I came away very disturbed. I told Charlie I was bothered by what went on between many of the couples. Although I couldn't put my finger on anything specific that was said and done, I told Charlie that I didn't think some of the couples belonged together. Time has proved me right. At least three of

the couples I wondered about have split up. How did I know? Was it body language?

It's very likely that you did pick up disturbing messages between these ill-suited couples. There is no doubt that people can send all sorts of emotional messages through body movement and tone of voice. A study was done by two psychologists, Drs. Ernst G. Beier and Daniel P. Sternberg, to look at just how much body language newlyweds use to communicate with each other.

Using fifty couples, the doctors gave each a psychological interview to find out how much conflict there was in the marriage. At the same time hidden cameras recorded the couples' body language toward each other.

Once the researchers found out which couples were having trouble and which had relatively peaceful marriages, they showed the videotapes of the interviews to experts in nonverbal communication and asked them to rate each couple on body language interaction.

Specifically, the experts looked for the presence or absence of eye contact, laughter, talking, touching, and the way the couples held their bodies, if their legs and arms were closed or open, if they leaned toward or away from each other.

The conclusion the researchers drew after matching the experts' reports with their own psychological interviews was that body language expressed a person's feelings very accurately. The "happy" couples would sit closer together, Dr. Beier said, "look more frequently into each other's eyes and touch each other more often than they touched themselves."

According to Dr. Beier, the couples experiencing the most conflict crossed their arms and legs, avoided eye contact with each other, and touched themselves more than they touched their partners. Obviously, in your church group, you received and interpreted all these signals correctly and were able to spot the couples with trouble in their future.

In following up his couples years later, Dr. Beier reported some interesting discoveries. If the wife in a marriage is dissastisfied, the couple is far more unhappy than they are if the husband is dissatisfied. As a rule, husbands had the same number of complaints as time went on. Not so the wives. They complained more and more as the marriage developed. He concluded that women expect a great deal out of a marriage—but don't get much. Men expect little in the first place, and they aren't disappointed when they don't get more!

Fred is a constant cigar smoker, and when I see him talking with a woman at a cocktail party, it seems to me that the way he handles his cigar should give me some clue to how he feels about her.

There are two ways in which you can interpret the body language of smokers. One is in the tactile range. A man's interest in a woman is often reflected in the way he handles a cigar or cigarette when he's with her. If he holds it gently, rolling it between his fingers, he may be unconsciously caressing a substitute for the girl.

A second approach may give you an insight to Fred's mood. The jaunty angle of his cigar as he approaches a girl he likes may demonstrate confidence, interest, and masculinity. A downcast cigar reverses the image.

The cigar can also be used as an extension of Fred's arm or hand to invade a woman's zone of privacy, to make her conscious of his closeness, to throw her slightly off balance and—with luck—to arouse her interest. Fred can use the same extension of hand and cigar to fence in a woman, to close a circle around her and cut her off from the rest of the company.

The danger Fred runs—as all smokers do—is that his partner may be allergic to the smoke or the odor of a cigar or cigarette and what he's trying to use as a positive sign will become a turn-off!

My wife and I were at a party the other day, and I was sitting and talking to one of the women for a while. Afterward, my wife said, "You really like her, don't you?" And I was surprised, because I couldn't figure out how she knew. When I asked her, she just looked puzzled and said, "I don't know why, but I can always tell if you like a person by the way you sit when you're with them." What body language signals tell her how I feel?

When you know a person for a long time, you often read their body language without knowing how you do it. This might have been what happened with your wife. The fact that you were interested in another woman probably made her reading all the more perceptive.

To dispel the mystery, you should be aware that sitting postures can give some revealing clues to likes and dislikes. When a man likes the woman he's talking to, he usually leans forward in a relaxed way with his back curved, assuming an attentive posture. If he dislikes the woman, he'll tend to slouch back in his chair as if to say "I'm just not interested enough to lean forward." Of course, the same postures apply to liking or interest between two men or two women.

Another indication of liking is curving the trunk toward the other person, opening your arms toward her, and crossing your legs in her direction. This is as indicative of interest as folding the arms across the chest while you lean back is indicative of resistance and disagreement.

My girfriend and I were out walking the other day in real muggy kind of weather, and she accused me of being very cold. She didn't mean I felt cold, she said, but that I wasn't smiling as much as I usually do. Also I was very uptight. Can the weather affect my body language?

The weather can affect almost anything in life, from the externals—such as picnics and outings—to the internals—such as how you feel. Barometric pressure can inflame our joints and cause etreme pain when we move. Sometimes, however, the pain is minimal. We may not be consciously aware of it, but still our movement, our body language, is restricted. We become less outgoing and withdraw more into ourselves.

As a scientific fact to lend authenticity to the effect of weather on body language, a research study done with hidden cameras on cloudy, sunny, and rainy days, concluded that in bad weather people talked to each other less, smiled less, and used more restricted body language.

But we don't really need scientific studies to tell us this. We all know that a gloomy day affects us and depresses us, while a mild, sunny day exhilarates us.

Your girfriend was simply stating a basic truth about the weather and body language—or how people feel.

We had an old college girlfriend of mine to dinner the other night, and when she left my husband said, "That lady's available!" I was very shocked, and I asked him how he knew. "By the way she was sitting with her legs open" was his answer. Is this true?

Ever since my book *Body Language* was published, people have asked me what various specific gestures mean. The truth is that every gesture has meaning only in terms of the total person. For some women, open legs indicate an open personality, closed legs a social and sexual tightness. But many other factors must be taken into consideration before judging such personality aspects.

When a woman wears pants, she can sit as she pleases. With a short skirt, she must sit a certain way, usually with her legs together at the thighs.

Sometimes closed arms mean resistance: "I don't want to hear you." I saw a picture of Dr. Benjamin Spock addressing a group of police recruits. The picture showed every policeman sitting with tightly crossed arms. Unquestionably knowing the the way both Dr. Spock and the police think, they were resisting what he had to say. But crossed arms do not always indicate resistance. Some people simply find it more comfortable to stand that way, and they may be very receptive to what you are saying though their arms are crossed. Again, you must consider the total person and the little messages you get from the rest of his posture.

Stroking the nose with one finger is held to be the preliminary to some outrageous statement or to a lie. But when someone suffers from hay fever, the nose wipe may simply be a way of relieving an itch!

Before you interpret body language gestures, you should understand the entire context of the situation. Your college friend, sitting with open legs, may simply have an open personality or an open mind. It doesn't necessarily follow that she's available.

My girlfriend always seems to be sending me a message in the way she crosses her legs, but I must be body-language-blind, because I just can't read it. Is there really a language of the legs?

Most serious students of body language feel that we have to be very cautious in reading any signals from leg placement unless we know the person thoroughly. Other, more irreverent women-watchers see an erotic language in the way legs are crossed.

If there were such a language, it would have to have been learned recently in historical terms, because it's only since the coming of short skirts and pants that we've been able to see women's legs clearly. It is also interesting to note that every attempt to study the erotic language of legs is applied to women, never to men! Even so, because of the amount of interest in the subject, it's probably worth seeing what the leg-watchers think.

In a recent article, clinical psychologist John A. Blazer analyzed what women say with their legs.

Dr. Blazer divided women into seven distinct types based on how they position their legs while sitting. *The organizer* is turned on by neatness and order, and she can be spotted by the parallel way in which she holds her legs. *The Schemer* is ambitious and competitive. She crosses above the knees and dangles one shoe, flirting but rarely delivering.

The conformist sits on one leg, and Dr. Blazer labels her a slow starter, but he says she likes being told what to do. *The perfectionist* crosses above her knees and twists her legs. She's supposed to be insecure and anxious, but sympathetic. *The social worker* crosses at the ankles and holds her knees apart. She's affectionate and generous if you're in trouble.

The emancipated woman keeps her legs wide apart, crossing at the calves, almost in a lotus position. She's "independent and unconventional." And lastly, *the philanthropist* holds her legs apart without crossing. She's "warm, easy going, and good humored."

How much of all this woman-watching and analysis has any basis in reality and how much is just fun and games? Well, there may be a one percent chance of accuracy in assessing character through sitting postures in both men and women without knowing them very well, but it's an iffy thing. Generally, open legs indicate an outgoing, free nature, closed legs a more repressed and inhibited attitude. Beyond these generalizations, it's a treacherous jungle of interpretation. Venture in at your own risk.

As far as sexual differences in crossing legs, men and women do cross differently—usually men in this country tend to cross their legs at a ninety-degree angle, with the ankle over the knee. Women usually keep their thighs close to parallel, the calf and ankle of the crossed leg below the knee of the other.

These differences may, in part, be due to differences in body structure between men and women and in part to differences in clothes. With her legs crossed, as a man's

is crossed, a woman in skirts feels more vulnerable and
open. In pants, she may well cross as a man crosses.

**I was in Italy recently, and I visited a number of
churches. In Ravenna, while I was examining a mosaic
of St. Luke, I was surprised to find that he had one
hand raised in a gesture that I know Italians use to
mean a wife has been cheating on a husband. What
significance can this gesture have in a religious picture?**

All body language gestures signal something in the context in which they are used. The same is true of the
spoken language. The word *err* means to make a mistake.
But if we use *er* as a pause filler—"I was—er—going to
the—er—store"—as many of us do, the listener knows what
we mean. He doesn't confuse *er* with *err,* even though
they are pronounced the same way.

The same is true of hand postures. They can signal one
thing in a certain context and something else in a different
context. The finger posture you noticed in the mosaic
of St. Luke is called, in Latin, the *Manu Cornuta,* and it
was commonly used to imply that a man was a cuckold
—at least up until the seventeenth century. Now its use
is rare, and mixed. Sometimes it is an insult, and sometimes it is a gesture of protection.

To make the *Manu Cornuta,* the two middle fingers
and the thumb are tucked into the palm. The little finger
and the index finger are pointed as if they were horns.

Originally, this was a pre-Christian gesture—in fact, a carved hand in this pose was found in the ruins of Herculaneum, the Italian city buried by Mount Vesuvius. Later, the early Christians used the sign as a protection against the evil eye and generally to banish evil. This was probably how it was meant in the Italian mosaic you saw.

Another hand gesture with historical significance is the *Manu Pantea,* in which all the fingers except the index and the one next to it are closed. These two are extended together or in a V angle. This sign had a special significance in early Greek and Roman times. It was used in tombs and carvings to mean a wise man, a judge, or a teacher. Later it became the benediction sign of Christianity. It signaled V for victory in World War II, and then in the sixties it became the peace sign.

There are fascinating historical backgrounds to various other hand postures, and, in an article called "The Communicative Hand," Dr. J. A. V. Bates of the National Hospital for Nervous Disease in London traces many of them. In a very original bit of research, he follows the history of a little-studied gesture he calls the 101. It's a hand with all fingers extended and spread except for the two middle ones, between the index and the little finger. These two are held touching. Try it. It's a difficult an unnatural gesture.

Dr. Bates finds it first in church mosaics made in the tenth century in Palermo. One of the fathers of the church, St. Basil, holds his hands in this position, and so does the Virgin Mary in many of her portraits. In many crucifixes it can be seen in the hand of Christ.

It disappears after the thirteenth century and appears again in the fifteenth in the hands of the baby Jesus and the Virgin in paintings from the Netherlands. Evidently it has been used all this time as a godlike gesture.

In the work of later painters, Botticelli and Bellini, the hand in this position began to appear on saints, and later Raphael used it in lesser characters in paintings in the Sistine Chapel.

It was then picked up in portraits. Titian used it for the repentent Mary Magdalene, and Bronzini gave it to hands in many paintings of men and women. Abbate, of the Fountainbleau school, gave the 101 hand posture to a brothel madam and a lecherous client of the brothel. The signal had lost all its holy, godlike meaning.

Today, Bates points out, he has seen it on a mannequin in the window of a Carnaby Street clothing store and in a poster for the play *Jesus Christ Superstar,* where Christ uses it to hold a microphone. Has it come full circle?

Last week I brought Sandra home to meet my folks. Sandra and Mom hit it off well, but both of them have this thing in common—fat! Mom is twice the weight she should be, and Sandra is coming along fast. Afterward, Mom kept at me about how great Sandra is,

always smiling. When I made some crack about her
weight, Mom laughed it off and said, "Well, you'll be
happy with her. Fat people are jolly by nature." Now
I'm not so sure that Sandra is all that jolly. Do fat people
really smile more and are they happier?

Your mother seems to confuse smiling a lot with being
happy or jolly, but there may be some logic at the root
of your confusion. The jolly fat person is so much a
stereotype that there has to be some truth to it. The
trouble is, the jolliness, the smilling, and the joking of
fat people are usually a defense, a way of saying "Like
me even though I'm fat and unattractive. I can still
make you laugh."

In a sense, they are trying to buy affection with a smile
because they feel so uncertain of their own physical
attractiveness. If this is where Sandra's at, then you're
right in your feeling that she's not all that jolly.

However, not all fat people smile, nor are they all
jolly. Many are just as serious, just as unhappy, and just
as unpleasant as their leaner cousins. There is nothing
in the physical makeup of a fat person to incline him
to jolliness. The clue lies in his psychological makeup.
The body language message he sends out is usually one
of desperation, a mask to cover up the hurt dealt to him
by a unsympathetic world.

In some cases, such people stay fat for these very
reasons, to create a mask to hide their inner selves. "If you

never see the real me, you can't hurt that me," they seem to be saying, as they hide behind their layers of fat.

If Sandra is like that and you truly love her, your good feelings for her and your respect for her as a person behind the fat may help her control her mixed-up image.

I'm twenty-two years old, just average in looks, and a little overweight, but I always seem to have more boys around than I can handle. My father says it's because I have sexy blue eyes—but I haven't, really! I've looked at my eyes in a mirror and in my photos, and all I can see that's different are large pupils. Could this be sexy?

Sexy is different things to different people. It's very possible that your eyes communicate warmth and softness because of the pupil size, but it's also possible that it's not your eyes but your personality that's responsible for the overabundance of boys.

As for the eyes—Dr. Eckhard H. Hess, professor of psychology at the University of Chicago, has come up with some convincing proof that pupil size in women can cause different attitudes in men. In an experiment, he showed two photographs of a pretty young woman to a group of men. Both photographs were identical, but in one the woman's pupils had been retouched so that they were larger. In the other they were made smaller.

How did the men react?

None of them noticed the pupil difference consciously, but all described the picture of the woman with the large pupils as soft, more feminine, and pretty.

The same woman with small pupils was seen as hard, selfish, or cold.

These results were more obvious when the woman had blue eyes.

It seems clear that large pupils make a woman more attractive to men, no matter what the woman is really like. Perhaps blue eyes emphasize the difference. Your father, in calling your eyes sexy, is simply putting into slang his feelings that you are pretty, warm, and feminine.

There's very little new under the sun, and for hundreds of years women have arrived at Dr. Hess's conclusion empirically. They've used the drug belladonna (which contains atropine) to make their eyes more beautiful. Atropine dilates the pupils of the eyes.

There are additional fascinating facts that Dr. Hess's work and the work of others have turned up about pupil size and people. Younger people have larger pupils than older people, and youth is usually more physically attractive.

Large pupils indicate interest on the part of the person who has them. Work done in this field (the new and growing science of pupillometry) shows that in men and women the pupil expands when we look at something we like. It's easy to conclude that the person who looks at you with large pupils likes you. We find people who like us much more attractive than people who don't. Is this why we like people with large pupils?

Men's pupils dilate when they see a woman with large pupils, but their pupils do not change when they look at other men with either large or small pupils. However, many women's pupils grow larger when they look at another woman with small pupils! Do these women prefer other women who seem cold, or are women with small pupils less of a challenge?

Two experimenters in pupillometry at the University of Missouri dilated the pupils of a man by using eyedrops and found that that he was preferred as a partner by both men and women—at least when they had to choose between him and a nondilated-eye partner.

At the University of Toronto, pupillometrists found that male homosexuals prefer women with small pupils. A final and thought-provoking finding at Toronto was that heterosexual Don Juans who wanted sex with many women, rather than a relationship with just one, have the same pupil response to women as homosexuals have. Are these men unconscious homosexuals? Or are they attracted by seemingly cold women who are less likely to be permanent partners?

My Aunt Grace used to be on the stage, and she always played very sexy parts. The thing is, now she's over seventy years old and you'd never know it. When I kid her about it, she just grins and says it's all in

her body. How can she use her body language to make herself look younger?

Your aunt knows that body language is at the very core of acting. A talented, twenty-five-year-old actor can walk on stage and project a man of eighty without saying a single word. He does it all with his body.

In Tom Stoppard's play *Travesties,* actor John Wood did an amazing transformation from a very young man to a very old one. Part of the trick was in his voice, but a greater part of it was in the way he used his body.

Conversely, a good, older actor can project youth with his body movement. I was on a television talk show once with Gloria Swanson, who is definitely getting on in years, yet she projected the image of a very young woman.

In part, she did it by covering her body completely. A pants suit and a long-sleeved blouse with a very high neck, bracelets to take the eyes off her hands, and an enormous hat to hide part of her face all helped. Dark glasses were the final touch. The body image she projected could have been any age from thirty on.

The real illusion started with her voice. It was firm and unwavering. She never groped for a word. But the greatest part of the youth she projected was in her body movement. She moved like a young woman and sent out a constant subliminal message: "I am young, young,

young!" Your Aunt Grace, in her movements and walk, probably projects the same message.

My wife has very large eyes, and we've both heard that this is a sign of an overemotional person. She's really troubled by this label because she feels that she's pretty level-headed. I know she is, but is there any truth in the saying?

Not a bit. The linking of large eyes to emotion, thin lips to meanness, and other physical features to personality is a type of character analysis that has been discredited by every sound scientific study. In spite of this, the myths persist, and there are even current books that play upon the fallacy.

The size and shape of your features, or, for that matter, of your body, feet, or hands, do not reflect your inner personality. There is no genetic link between appearance and character.

How you move your body and your features is another story. We are all born with differently shaped eyes, and we can hold them at various levels and project different expressions with them. We can hold our mouths differently, become tight-lipped or project one lip over another, jut out our jaws or slump our bodies—but these are ways in which the personality affects the way we use our features.

The way we hold our face can even determine beauty

or ugliness. Just think of some of our plastic-faced comedians who can change character just by puffing out their cheeks or loosening their lips, widening their eyes or raising their eyebrows.

One important point to remember in all of this is that your appearance, or your own concept of how you look, whether you think you're beautiful or ugly, can influence your personality. People treat good-looking men and women differently, and this difference can have an effect.

If your wife had been told that big eyes meant an emotional nature ever since she was a child, she might well have become overemotional to live up to the expectations of others, just as red haired people often are conned into believing that they have very short tempers. It's expected of them, and they fall into the trap.

Usually Selma is a very ordinary-looking woman, but I've known her for years, and I've lived through her love affairs with her. I know for a fact that she actually looks prettier when she's in love. How is this possible?

It is not only posible, but it usually happens. There is a very strong connection between the body and the mind. The connection is called *psychosomatic,* and usually we think of it in terms of illness. A person's mind can influence his body to make him sick or well. A sick or healthy body, in turn, can influence the mind.

The connection is not mysterious. It is based on the

nervous system and the different chemical hormones that flood the body at the command of the mind. These hormones direct the actions of glands and blood vessels.

When Selma falls in love, her emotional reactions cause an unconscious response in her body and in her body language. Her muscle tone is heightened, and the sagging lines in her face are tightened up. Her skin may flush more readily, and her eyes may sparkle while her poor posture disappears.

A number of courting signals are released at a time like this, and all in all a body language message is sent out: "I am attractive and desireable." The message influences the fact. Selma becomes prettier.

My uncle and aunt are a very close couple. They are always together, and when you ask one a question, the other can, as likely as not, answer. They think that much alike. But what's really far out is that every day my uncle seems to look a little more like my aunt! I've been wondering: Do people who live together really get to look like each other?

Oddly enough, this is one folk tale that apparently has some truth to it. People who live together and like each other often begin to do the same things, to think alike, and to react in the same way, as your uncle and aunt do. Eventually, they aquire similar habits and similar reactions. They begin to develop the same characteristics.

I know one divorced mother who says her daughter always looks much more like her father after a week's visit with him. The daughter looks very much like her father to begin with, but after being with him for a week she begins to hold the muscles of her face (when she laughs, smiles, blinks, frowns, etc.) much more the way her father does.

We are all born with unique features, but there is a certain plasticity to everyone's face. We can all do the same things with our mouths, eyes, and noses. We can smile, frown, sneer, grimace, and go through the hundreds of facial expressions everyone else goes through.

To a large extent, as the poets have it, the face is the mirror of the soul. Like the portrait of Dorian Gray, our faces reflect what goes on inside us, and they are influenced by our expressions.

For this reason, people who share common experiences, as your uncle and aunt do, will often begin to react the same way and develop the same wrinkles, lines, and expressions—in short, they will eventually look alike.

Last week I just about decided that I had had it with this city. It's not the crowds—I can take them—but it's the touching in the crowds! I'm not any prettier than the next woman, but it seems to me that whenever I'm out on a bus or shopping the men are always touching me. What gives them the right to do this?

The right to touch someone else in our society seems to go hand in hand with status. Those people who are richer, older, and male have the social right to touch the ones who are poorer, younger, and female—at least this was the conclusion of a study by psychologist Nancy H. Henley of Harvard University.

Observing about one hundred public incidents of hand-to-shoulder, elbow-to-ribs, or any other touching pattern, Dr. Henley found that there were far more cases of men laying hands on women, than there were instances of women touching women, men touching men, or women touching men.

Once touched, Dr. Henley found, women were less likely to return the touch. Most men grabbed at a chance to touch back when a women touched them.

She also found that older people touched younger people more often than the younger touched the older, and richer people were more apt to touch poorer. Young men rarely touched back, but if they did, it was always a woman they touched.

Outdoors, twice as many men touched women as indoors. Were they counting on easy getaways if rebuffed? Women who touched men did it indoors as often as out.

What it all boils down to, Dr. Henley believes, is that men consider themselves superior to women and so see themselves with the right to touch them. The reason it happens more often outdoors, she explains, is that indoors a man can more easily show power with other body language gestures such as eye movements, gestures of the hands, and voice shifts.

Appalled that something as human as touch can be perverted to a symbol of status and power, Dr. Henley sadly admits that just as food, shelter, and clothing are unevenly distributed throughout the world, so it is, too, with the socially-doled-out right to touch.

I was watching a football game recently, and I noticed that after a successful play by one man, a teammate ran up and patted his rear end. I don't watch football often, and the gesture shocked me. It seemed so—well, sexual. I began to wonder about those two men. But when I mentioned it to my husband, he just laughed at me and said it goes on all the time in football and doesn't mean a thing. Is this true?

This is a symbolic body language gesture that lies very close to the danger area in man-to-man communication. What the gesture says, of course, is "Thanks for a great play!," and it says it in an expression of warmth, of touching, and of sexuality.

Does this mean that football players are potentially homosexual? It's not likely, because if a player were homosexual he'd be inhibited about the gesture and it isn't likely that he'd use it in public.

In our male culture, such gestures between men are

often done as a joke. It becomes a gesture of admiration, but a funny, sexual, symbolic one.

The constant body contact of a sport like football may also lead to greater body awareness among players. The pat on the rear is an acceptable way of discharging such awareness, as is the hugging after a successful play. But in most cases, these gestures are simply traditional. Others do it, the player figures, so I'll do it, too.

Another significance of these expressions is their reinforcement of male bonding. Some evolutionary psychologists feel that a long process of natural selection favored those men who hunted well together and were most comfortable in the company of other men. Primitive hunting was done best in groups, and therefore men who liked to hunt in groups had an edge in the struggle to survive. These psychologists reason that over the millennia a preference for the company of other men was bred into the males of the human race. This they call male bonding.

One woman I know who jogs with her husband tells me that occasionally, after a good workout, her husband gives her this "man-to-man" pat on the rear. She recognizes it for what it is: a sign from her husband that she is, for the moment, "one of the guys"—a sign that he accepts her in a situation that has traditionally been mostly male.

The comfort many men feel in the company of other men leads to these contact gestures. Among male adolescents, goosing is a favorite agressive-sexual-fun gesture, and it carries over into many societies of men alone, such as the army, all-male schools, and fraternities.

Your football player, with his intimate approval touch, may simply be reinforcing a genetic male bonding, a pleasure in the company of other men.

My husband and I have certain friends, a couple we've known for years and years and like very much. Recently they've suggested that all four of us go off together on a cruise. I'd like to, but the problem is the husband, Bob. He just can't keep his hands off me. He's a terrible toucher. Of course, it's not only me—he seems to touch everyone at parties and social evenings, even when his wife is around. What is he trying to tell us with all this contact.

Without knowing Bob and his background, nobody can say just why he has such a great tactile need. Dr. Theodore I. Rubin, who has written a good deal on psychological matters, suggests that for many touchers the presence of the wife may be just the thing that causes the problem. He feels that often excessive touchers are men rebelling against their mothers. They have made their wives into substitute mothers, and touching other women is a way of getting back at their own mothers—in the image of their wives.

With other men, the touching may be an attempt to manipulate and embarrass their wives. To act this way, they would have to be hostile to their wives on a deep level, Dr. Rubin adds. He believes that there are other men who touch excessively just to annoy the husbands of the women they touch. They feel this is masculine behavior.

Still another reason, he says, may be an unconscious contempt for women in general, a feeling that they are all there for his enjoyment, nice objects to be touched and fondled as he wishes.

Lastly, Dr. Rubin feels that some men use this touching for sexual stimulation and a substitute for more complete involvement.

In addition to the reasons given by Dr. Rubin, there may be a simpler, more acceptable explanation. Touch is a very basic means of communication. Children need touching and fondling in order to grow up into normal, healthy adults. If the touching is denied them in childhood, they often search for it in adult life.

Such a man, deprived of this basic need, can become an excessive toucher. The touching will have little sexual connotation, and a woman will be completely "safe"—if not at ease—in his presence.

Your problem with Bob might be easily solved if you could bring yourself to have a frank, but friendly, talk with him. You might even take a tip from the men in Greece and buy him a string of *worry* beads. Greek men fondle these smoothly shaped beads constantly as a means of discharging an excessive need for touching or an extra amount of anxiety.

**All the other girls at my school are beginning to go
braless, and I think they're right. I'm so much more
comfortable without one. But I tried it last week, and
my boyfriend, Leo, blew his stack. He claims this is a
signal that I'm available. I think he's out of his tree!
Do you agree?**

With the freedom in dress that women have demanded
and received in the last few years, my first impulse would
be to agree with you that Leo is indeed out of his tree.
I'd like to believe that most men are too liberated to
accept no bra as a sexual come-on. But the facts are more
disheartening.

Someone decided to find out just what going without
a bra did signal to young men, and a study was under-
taken at a group of colleges. Dozens of male students were
questioned, and, in an environment where the braless
style was the campus fashion, most male students still
thought girls without bras were:

1) horny
2) sexy
3) permissive
4) available
5) a sure thing

Leo was not as wrong as we both thought he was.
Reality evidently still has a long way to go before it
catches up with the traditional male fantasies!

Yesterday my husband and I went to an important civic dinner. I fell apart because I had nothing to wear, and before the evening was over I had a knock-down, drag-out fight with my husband. He claims I'm all hung up on what other women think of my clothes, and afterward I began to wonder just who I was dressing for. Do women dress for themselves, for other women, or for men?

Many psychologists believe that women dress not for other women nor for men, but for their own subconscious. If this is the case, a woman's clothes may be a subtle body language message that can reveal many things about her.

For example, a happily married woman may select extremely seductive clothes just to make her husband jealous, to make him aware that she can still attract other men. An obsession with such clothes can be a sign of a very basic insecurity about herself and a need to bolster her own ego.

A woman who gathers many more hats and pairs of shoes than she can logically use is often someone who is overweight and frustrated in her attempts to buy attractive clothes in her size. She settles for things like hats and shoes because shoe and hat size is no indication of her unhappy physical condition.

An extremely expensive wardrobe can be an unconscious boast to the world that a woman's husband is well-to-do and can support her. The husband usually goes along, secretly happy, though he feels the need to complain. After all, this kind of wife is an advertisement for his own success.

These reasons, of course, are not true for all women. As with all body communication, you can't generalize. Women's reasons for dressing the way they do are as varied as women's natures. But an awareness of the possible reasons we dress in a certain way may open our eyes to a greater understanding of ourselves.

I've always enjoyed spending my vacations at a nudist colony, and recently I convinced my girlfriend that she should go with me. She didn't enjoy it at all, and one of the reasons she gave was "I'm just not used to nude body language!" Is there such a thing? Are there any special body language rules for nudists?

I've spoken to many nudists, and all seem to find one common but unspoken law in operation. There is an exaggerated amount of eye contact among nudists, almost as if it were a defense against letting the eyes wander to more intimate areas of the body.

"This is not a conscious thing," one confirmed nudist stressed. "It's just something you do without realizing it. In a way, I guess it's a part of the overexaggerated respect for privacy that goes along with nudism."

Another one of "those things that go along with nudism" my friend tells me, is a lack of touching. "There is almost no touching in the average nudist colony." When pressed for his own explanation, he suggested that it might be a fear of arousal or a respect for privacy.

Among the other interesting observations he made during his years as a nudist:

In the beginning, a towel, even if it is held without covering the body, serves as a *pacifier*. Later, as a person becomes more at ease with nudism, the need for a pacifier disappears.

Fastidiousness cuts across all lines. A fastidious person remains that way whether dressed or nude.

The use of territorial space among nudists depends on their rapport with their neighbors rather than on their cultural background.

The intriguing thing about nudity, my friend reports, is that it does away with all status symbols. Short of hair-styles, beards, and moustaches, there is no way to identify the economic niche of the other person. It causes a curious kind of leveling.

However, some other nudist friends who favor the Riviera and the West Indies claim that suntan definitions are a type of status symbol. The narrower the band of pale skin around the hips in a man and around the hips and breast in a woman, the higher the status. The overall tan, however, is usually frowned on because without contrast there is no way of knowing how much is suntan and how much the pigment melanin.

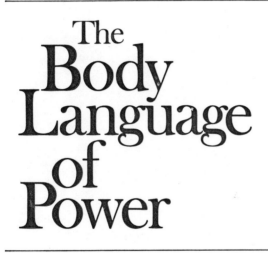

The
Body
Language
of
Power

My father-in-law is a lawyer, and yesterday I was in
his office when a new client came in. I've rarely seen
my father-in-law so respectful to anyone, and afterward
I asked why. He told me he knew the client was an
important and powerful man just by the way he walked
in. It turned out he was right, but I don't believe
anyone can tell this by a walk. What do you think?

I'm with your father-in-law. You can read quite a bit of
character from a man's walk. The hard walker is often a
determined person. The fast walker tends to be impatient

and aggressive. The way a man walks will reflect the way he uses his body—the way he uses his body can tell you the type of man he is.

By examining someone's walk, you get an overall impression of what that person is like, and this impression is often true. A tentative person will walk tentatively, almost questioning the ground at every step. A jaunty walker often turns out to be happy-go-lucky, and so on.

We really need no training to read a person's walk. A quick impression is received, and our mental computer automatically selects the descriptive word that applies: rich, happy, secure, powerful, uncertain, lonely, ill—all this can be seen in a walk.

When your father-in-law sees a man with a determined walk and senses a touch of arrogance in the way he carries his body, then he knows that man is powerful and inspires respect—at least in his eyes.

Last week I called on a new client, and his receptionist gave me a really hard time. I finally got through and made a decent sale, but I could have easily been scared off by her attitude. How can I gain the upper hand in situations like this? Is there any way that body language can help me past these dragons?

There are ways, but they won't work too well if you persist in seeing the receptionist as a dragon. You'll be on your way to a solution when you realize that if you haven't a firm appointment the way you relate to the receptionist will determine, to a big extent, whether you'll get in to see the client at all.

Your brush with the receptionist is a classic man-woman encounter. It embodies a certain amount of flirtation and a certain amount of hostility. Allow the flirtation to be strong and play down the obvious hostility you feel. Compliment her subtly by letting her know you admire her as a woman. Inevitably, this becomes a sexual "play," the mild, often unconscious, flirtation that takes place between a man and a woman in any situation.

The salesman must be aware of the sexual undercurrent and realize that it has its useful aspects—but also its dangerous ones. He can use it, but he must keep the encounter a business relationship, on a formal level.

What is needed is a simple disclaimer of any intention of following through on the flirtation. The disclaimer can be a touching of the wedding ring or the verbal mention of a wife and family. Even if it's very subtle it will be understood, because most often there is no real intention to go beyond a mild flirtation on either side, yours or the receptionist's.

What it all boils down to is the attitude you take. If you see her as a dragon, a guardian, or a hostile protector of her boss's office, you're going to resent her and your resentment will show through in your body language.

Look at her from a different viewpoint and see her as a pleasant woman who may be on your side, who may help you in to see the client. Your different attitude will reflect itself in your body language. She'll pick up the "vibes," and the entire encounter will become a pleasant one.

Does a woman in power have to make concessions in her dress and style to the prejudices of the organization she works for? For example, could a bank president go braless?

To project power, one must always be conscious of the prejudices of the group. The effectiveness of the projection of power depends upon how it is interpreted. For example, if you are the vice president of a woman's bank, going without a bra becomes a statement and is therefore a plus. But in a more conservative bank, a braless look could be misconstrued and could, therefore, diminish power.

Men in power, though, often find themselves in a similar predicament. Some large corporations frown upon their executives dressing casually.

Women and men both can project a powerful image regardless of how they dress. But in the business world, both must often make concessions in their dress to maintain an image of power.

I teach a group of nursery school children, and the other day Ronnie, one of my favorites, misbehaved. I tried

to act very stern with him, but he just smiled at me and went on doing what he pleased. It's almost as if he knows that I like him too much to really discipline him. Can a child Ronnie's age read my real feelings?

Children six years old and younger are very impressionable, and they can understand a body message that confirms or denies the spoken word. They have had experience with their own parents who will say one thing and then in body language communicate something entirely different, even contradictory.

All of us do this to children because we treat them with a constant hypocrisy. We tell them dozens of untruths from "the stork brought you," to "it's wrong to lie." They soon discover the stork had nothing to do with it, and they realize, from the moment they become rational, that lying is often a fact of life.

If a child couldn't sort out the truth from all the lies his parents told him, he would go quite mad. So early on, as a defense, he learns to read his parents' body language —a much truer type of communication. It tells him just what he can and can't get away with.

In school, the child carries this same ability to read the truth into his dealings with the teacher. As a teacher, you're very quickly sized up, judged, and tested by Ronnie. In his eyes you've failed the test. He knows you like him too much to punish him, no matter how stern you pretend to be. He reads your body language correctly and does as he pleases

I work for a man who always smiles, no matter what
the situation. Last month we lost our biggest account,
and when I told him about it he smiled even while
he was shaking his head and swearing! Now I wonder
Does he just not understand the situation, or can you
smile when you're unhappy? What do smiles mean?
What can they tell about a person?

A smile can be a wonderful source of communication—or
a mask that prevents communication. Your boss undoubtedly uses a smile as a mask, as something to hide his
true feelings or to give him a chance to collect his feelings. This is a very common mask, and many people use
it. The smile becomes automatic, a reaction to any situation. While the smile is on, the smiler can assess what's
happening, collect his thoughts, and keep control.

Jimmy Carter has this type of smile. Even when he's
confronted with an obvious problem, a wrong statement
he's made, or an untenable position he's taken, he responds
with a quick, nervous smile. The smile doesn't reflect his
true reaction but goes on as a quick mask while he collects
his thoughts. His next words will often completely
contradict the smile.

The key word with this type of smile is control. People
who use a smile as a mask are in constant control of
their emotions. They dread giving away a sincere and
honest part of themselves—how they really feel and react.
This would make them vulnerable, and for some people

being vulnerable is a frightening experience. If there is no one you trust, how can you allow yourself to be vulnerable at any time?

The smile as a mask is very much like the "professional" smile, the smile used by people who are constantly in the public eye. Jacqueline Onassis has such a smile—very practiced, very broad, almost frantic. But her eyes remain untouched. A normal smile, if it's broad, lifts the cheeks and crinkles the eyes. Jackie's smile doesn't touch the eyes. But neither do the smiles of most women who are very aware of their appearance. Carol Channing, Gloria Swanson, half the Hollywood crowd of actresses have learned to smile with their lips while keeping their eyes wide and open—pretty eyes in preference to honest eyes.

Then there are actresses who seem to say "To hell with how I look!" and who smile accordingly. Katharine Hepburn and Bette Midler are examples. When they smile, their whole face smiles.

What can you tell about a person from a smile? If the smile is genuine, it gives you a sudden glimpse of the inner person, the real man or woman. But if the smile is a mask or a professional smile, all it can tell you is that the person is concerned with appearances.

Psychologically, the greater the concern with appearance, the less inner strength and self-esteem a person has. Someone who is really self-assured won't bother to mask his feelings.

I was making a sales pitch to the buyer for a large department store the other day, and I thought things were going very well, but halfway through it he yawned. He told me he was up late the night before, but I couldn't help thinking it was my pitch that bored him. How can I tell when to keep pressing toward a sale —or when I should quit while I'm ahead?

When the average customer listens to a sales pitch, he attempts, very consciously, to prevent any emotion from showing on his face. There's a common feeling that if you let a salesman see how his pitch moves you—positively or negatively—you give him a certain advantage. With this attitude, even if your pitch is great, the customer won't show how impressed he is.

In spite of this, a good deal of your customer's true feelings will be betrayed by his face. No matter how hard he tries to keep a noncommittal look, part of the truth will leak through.

Slow-motion picture studies of people's faces, when they try to cover up their emotions, show momentary flickers of the truth, of the emotions they really feel, disgust, anger, boredom, annoyance. These are just flickers that pass so rapidly that the untrained eye cannot sort them out. But a part of your brain does observe them and record them, even though it all happens too fast for conscious recognition. These records are fed into the computer of our minds, and we react to the hidden message.

A good salesman has a natural talent for reading these subliminal messages. They tell him when he's on the wrong track or the right one, and they help him select the right sales pitch.

It is possible to train yourself in this technique and improve your own ability to pick up these fleeting clues. You first must become aware that they exist and that heightened awareness will aid your perception.

This takes a great deal of practice, and the practice can't be done on a client. Your mind would be so concerned with getting and reading subliminal signals that you would have nothing left over to concentrate on the sale.

Your best bet is to let your unconscious take over. If you feel your client is bored—go with your intuition. Intuition is simply your own mental computer sizing up and rejecting or accepting.

My little girl is only three years old, but she has a mind of her own. She can twist her father around her little finger, and she has an uncanny ability to second-guess me. Can this be because she reads our body language?

She probably does. In many cases children are more aware of and more tuned in to body language than adults are.

They are quick to understand a body language message that contradicts the spoken one.

My friend had a four-year-old son who was an expert at this. His parents were in the process of getting a divorce and were doing their best to keep their true feelings from their son.

One day his mother came into Billy's room and found him packing his toys carefully into a large cardboard carton he had picked up outside.

"What are you doing?" she asked.

Billy shrugged. "When you and Dad stop living with me and I have to leave, I want to have my toys all packed."

She sat down with him and talked for a while, and to her surprise found that he was convinced they'd separate soon. "But we never mentioned it to him," she protested later. Neither of us ever let him know how we felt. How could he guess?"

To Billy it wasn't a guess. His parents had been sending very obvious messages, and he was able to read them.

This uncanny ability to see through adult lies and read their true feelings in their body language is the reason many children will deliberately disobey a request or an order from their parents. The spoken comand is one thing, but behind it lies the unspoken, unconscious message which often tells them, "I won't be terribly mad if you do it." Or even, "I really want you to do it!"

Your own daughter probably reads your husband clear enough to know she won't be punished for what she does.

I went to apply for a job recently, and, without thinking
I put on a dress that I don't like. I felt more and more
uncomfortable in it during the day, and by time I
had my job interview I literally felt a mess. P.S.—I didn't
get the job! Could that dress have been responsible?

It could, or, to be more honest, your attitude toward the
dress could have killed the job interview. Not only do
clothes make the man, or woman, but sometimes—as in
your case—they can unmake him or her.

The image we project to the world around us is also
the image we project inward. If we are dissatisfied with
that image, we are ultimately dissatisfied with ourselves.
Our face and figure as well as our clothes make statements
about ourselves and how we feel about ourselves. Often
that statement is not what we wish it to be. It falls short
of our expected self-image, and in turn we feel that
somehow we've failed. We are simply not sending the
message we'd like to send.

The clothes we wear define us in a dozen different ways.
Alice likes to project a cosmopolitan image, and the little
status symbols of designer initials on her dress, yellow
fleur-de-lis on her plastic bag, gold metal Vs on her
Valentino shoes all work to assure her that she's a person
of taste and knowledge. She walks with assurance and
signals that assurance in an interview or on a date.

Jane, on the other hand, wants to make a completely
different statement. She favors bleached jeans and T-shirts
and declares, "My life-style is casual." The success of her

statement in the eyes of the people she meets feeds back to strengthen her own attitude.

The lesson? For a job interview, or for that matter in any situation in which you want to take charge, make sure you're comfortable in what you wear. If you really feel sure of yourself, you'll project that feeling. If you feel a mess, you'll project that, too!

Jim is the most successful salesman in our office, and I've been watching his body language to see if I could pick up a few pointers. So far, the only thing I've noticed is that he nods constantly when someone talks to him. Do you think this mannerism is part of Jim's success?

It may well be. When two people are in agreement and they talk together, there are often rhythmic body language movements that both fall into. When you are really getting your point across and the other fellow thinks you're right, his movements will often match yours in a kind of synchrony. This is the point of complete agreement.

Your successful salesman, Jim, by nodding when someone talks to him, signals, "I'm with you. I agree with your point of view." In turn, this can loosen up his client who will begin to move in synchrony. A feeling of warmth and understanding can be developed in this manner.

This may be a large factor in Jim's success, even if he is not consciously aware of what he's doing. To do this on a conscious level takes a great deal of skill and subtlety. If his nodding becomes too blatant and obvious, he can blow the entire sale.

I'm a manager in a large department store, and I feel very sympathetic to the men and women who work under me, but there must be something about my attitude that prevents them from trusting me. Is there any way I could use body language to communicate my own attitude to these people and convince them that I'm on their side?

You may be putting off your fellow workers by the expression on your face. Does a smile come easy? Try it. Try more eye contact.

A feeling of liking or warmth is best communicated through touching. Sometimes a handshake held a bit longer than necessary, a firm handshake, a touch on a person's shoulder—if done naturally—can say, "I like you. I want to communicate better."

Of course, too much touching can send an uncomfortable message. There are some people who hate to be touched. But a wise man very quickly learns how to gauge the reaction of the person he touches.

How a manager manipulates the space between himself and his subordinates also says a great deal about his attitude. On your own home ground, your office, the desk can often act as a barrier betwen you and someone who works for you. By arranging the office so that the visiting worker sits on one side of the desk while the manager sits on the other, the manager automatically proclaims himself the leader. He exaggerates the distance between them.

However, if he places the visitor's chair near the corner of his desk, or along the side facing him, he minimizes the barrier and indicates that he and the worker are equal.

If the office is too small for such an arrangement, the manager can come around the desk to be on the same side as his visitor—and abolish the barrier. He might sit on the desk, adopting an informal attitude—close to his visitor, but, since he is the ranking person, higher than his visitor, dominating the situation.

Another tip: If the manager wants to make the subordinate insecure, he'll summon him to his office. If he wants to reassure him, he'll visit the subordinate's office.

An aware manager will often temper his messages with body language. When he's criticizing a worker, he might touch him, as if to say, "Don't feel too bad. In spite of my criticism I still like you.

On the other hand, when he praises a worker, he might avoid body contact, withdrawing slightly, sending the message, "You're doing well. But don't let it go to your head!"

**I recently started working as a salesman for a large
company. I think they have a great line of goods, and I
really want to do my best at this job. How can I stay
in control in a selling situation? Can body language be
of any help in bettering the relationship between me
and the customer?**

Body language can be one of the salesman's best
friends. From the moment you enter your client's office,
even before you speak, there will be body language signs
from him that will clue you in to his mood and give you
some hints on how to act.

Watch the way he sits and stands. Does his body
seem tight, his movements spastic? Or is he open and
relaxed? Does he tend to touch you, or does he avoid
your touch? How does he shake hands? How far away
does he like to sit?

These are all clues, and the salesman who learns to read
them has a greater chance of adjusting his own body
language accordingly and slanting his sales pitch to overcome the client's resistance.

In terms of your own actions, decide whether you want
to dominate the man you're selling to or let him dominate
you. There are obvious advantages to the latter. He will
feel more confident and be apt to let his guard down.
He may also be more receptive if he thinks he has the
upper hand.

One salesman I know is well over six feet tall, but

whenever he enters a buyer's office he finds some way of sitting a little lower than his customer.

"Sometimes I have to slouch to do it," he explained to me. "But I try never to give him the feeling that I'm looming over him. That makes a man nervous and edgy. I want my guy relaxed and receptive."

Another body language clue is the way you sit. Someone wisely said that no salesman ever made a sale leaning back in a chair. By leaning forward you signal a degree of intensity and interest, of confidence in your product.

Of course, in adapting any of these gestures to your own actions, you run a certain risk. The "natural" salesman does all of these things unconsciously. They are a part of his selling personality. If you're going to attempt them when you don't honestly believe in what you're selling, then a part of that disbelief will show through in unconscious body betrayals.

With this in mind, most teachers of good salesmanship first attempt to teach genuine enthusiasm. Believe in what you sell and you'll convince your client.

They're right, of course. You must believe unless you're an excellent con man. If you don't believe, you must sell yourself before you sell anyone else. If you do believe, then all you need do is be aware of a few basic body language points such as body zones, dominance and posture. The rest will all fall into place by itself.

You are in a good position since you already think that your firm has a great line of goods. You've taken the first step.

My boss frequently comes to the office wearing his tennis clothes. Is this his way of showing how important he really is?

Yes. Dressing "against the grain" in a calculated way whether for an actual event such as a tennis game, or just for effect (such as Howard Hughes's tennis shoes), is indeed part of power symbolism. Another example is the rich man who flaunts the frayed overcoat.

Women play the power game in clothing somewhat differently, tending toward expensive symbols such as the Louis Vuiton handbag.

Dressing "against the grain" in an office situation tends to be much more a man's game than a woman's. What it all adds up to is an unspoken statement: I'm a powerful person, and I can dress any way I choose to.

Our sales force recently had a meeting to discuss selling methods, and one of the men insisted that the first impression we make on a customer is the way we enter his office. He claims that before we even open our mouths, an opinion has been formed about us. Is he right?

Entering an office can be a power game in itself. Do you knock and wait to be asked in? Do you knock and walk right in? Do you come in without knocking? The last is the most dominating entrance, the first is the least.

How do you enter? Do you hesitate at the door and wait until you're asked to sit down? Do you come halfway to your client's desk and wait to be offered a seat? Do you come up to the desk, shake hands, and sit in any available seat? Again, the first is the least dominant, the last the most.

But the obvious question is, do you want to dominate the situation when you come to sell something? Or do you want to give the impression of not dominating, even when you are?

The first impression, after the power ploy of the entrance, should come from the total look of the salesman: his clothes, his physical appearance, whether he has a beard or a moustache.

After the total impression, the customer becomes aware of the way the salesman carries himself: his posture, his gestures, how he moves.

Gestures can be very important—in a negative way. Tugging at an earlobe, chewing a lip, playing with the hair, beard, or moustache all transmit a message: "I am ill at ease."

The initial customer reaction will be, "Can I trust his product?"

The good salesman learns to control his body. He sums up the body language of his customer and then adapts his own to match it, but before he does this he sends out a message of his own. His entrance, his appearance, his gestures all go to make up that message.

My new job is great. I'm a troubleshooter for a big manufacturing outfit, and I'm on the move a lot, getting together with new people every week. My problem is that I get very nervous when I meet someone for the first time. Are there any body language tricks to keep me from showing this nervousness?

It's interesting that you ask for a way of covering up your nervousness rather than doing away with it. Evidently you recognize a very important point, that a slight amount of anxiety helps you to cope with a situation. Too much, of course, is harmful. But a small amount can improve your performance.

The most revealing parts of the body are the hands. They will often give you away with nervous gestures, and the best method of avoiding this betrayal is to find something for your hands to do. Smoking is the most obvious "busy" work for uneasy hands, but that cure may be worse than the disease. Besides, too many people are offended by smoking.

Many people use elaborate routines with pencils, notebooks, and eyeglasses—little rituals of movement—to absorb their nervousness. I know a man who carries a pipe into business conferences. He never gets around to smoking it, but he has dozens of preparatory gestures, filling and tamping and cleaning, that allow him to use his hands and his eyes. Eye contact, too, can betray and arouse nervousness, and a legitimate way of limiting it can help hide your nervousness.

Any of these rituals for your hands and eyes are best rehearsed before so that they don't become nervous mannerisms themselves

The other side of the coin is that you can use your understanding of these nervous gestures to detect uneasiness in others. It's up to you if you wish to allay someone else's discomfort—or use it for your own ends. At any rate, concentrating on other peoples' reactions will smooth out your own.

I was just promoted to a supervisory position in our plant. It's a great opportunity, but I'm having problems dealing with the people under me. I can't seem to undersand when they're accepting me or when they're resisting me. Is there some way a better understanding of body language could help me?

Absolutely. Even partially understood body language can help. For one thing, reading a subordinate's body messages correctly can help you decide whether he's tense or relaxed. If your subordinate is uncomfortable, you'll have to take a different approach in supervising him—particularly if the message you want to get across is going to be hard to take.

What are the clues to look for? Well, the uptight person often reveals his nervousness in a rigid, guarded stance. A typically resistant posture consists of arms folded tightly across his chest, a grim face, and a tense body.

He may betray his rigidity with lips pressed together, eyebrows lowered, and quick, jerky movements. Frequently, he won't raise his eyes to meet yours.

The relaxed person has a general looseness about his body and a comfortable stance and movement.

It's easy to spot either an uncomfortable person or a relaxed one, once you know what you're looking for. The next step is to learn to project either quality yourself in order to put the person at ease or on the defensive, depending on which suits your purpose best.

I just got a job in a large data-processing outfit, and I find the work fascinating. But one thing about this outfit bugs me. All of us are required to follow rigid dress codes—short hair and business suits for men and dresses for the women. What does all this accomplish anyway?

For one thing, it creates an image for the organization. The workers project a standardized message. In a giant corporation which must exude confidence and security, the message is "We hire a neat, businesslike worker, the kind you can trust to be sensible and level-headed." By implication, the company can also be trusted.

In contrast, a clothing store that sells mainly to young people may want to create a youthful "with it" image. The salesmen may be encouraged to wear long hair and far-out clothes. The image projected is not solidity, but the now generation.

We might think of these latter working conditions as freer, but the young salesman in this clothing store who wanted to wear a gray flannel suit and a tie instead of work shirt and jeans would be under the same pressure to conform as the corporation worker who tried to wear jeans instead of a suit.

That may be so, but if an established organization like mine promotes such rigidity in dress, aren't all of us workers going to be equally rigid in our thinking?

Possibly, and this can create a problem, too. In big business, management often needs innovative people with imagination and originality. But the workers are trained to conform not only in clothing but in thinking as well. These workers become of little value in the hunt for new talent. As a result, management frequently goes outside its own organization to recruit.

However, there are always a few mavericks in any corporation, a few men and women who refuse to fit into the corporate mold. They are free agents in clothes and ideas—and often they lose their jobs for that very reason.

But a few of them, if they are original and productive, can fight the corporate stifling and get ahead. In doing so, they may make such a reputation for themselves that management will search them out when it needs bright, talented thinkers. It doesn't happen often, but in a sense it's big business's only salvation to advance these people. Wily and intelligent personnel managers will search their own ranks for just such maverick talent.

I'm a manager in a large corporation, and my work load is tremendous. Most of my day is spent in my own office or in conference with other executives. I see nothing unusual in this, but recently my secretary has made some remarks about my not really knowing the workers in my department. Will being closer to the workers diminish the authority I have over them?

In big business, there is usually a very definite separation between worker and executive, and the separation has its advantages on both sides. An executive can be tougher with his subordinates when he is not personally involved with them, and a worker can make stronger demands if he is not a friend of the executive.

However, there are very definite advantages to a certain amount of worker-boss communication. In those industries where the employer is kept totally apart from the worker, there is more apt to be an uneasy feeling, a sense of discomfort, especially in times of business stress.

Studies show this uneasiness can be overcome if the employer makes himself "available" to the workers, even if it's only a visual availability. His office should not be so separate that it becomes a virtual no man's land. He should achieve some contact by walking through the plant often enough to be a familiar sight to the workers.

The situation you describe, of spending all your time in your own office or with management on your own level, is a very awkward one. You should try to overcome it with a higher degree of visibility. Get to know something of the men under you, and take the time to talk to them, even if it's a brief word or two. And most important, do it by going to them rather than summoning them to your office.

A top executive at an advertising agency told me that he makes it a point, at least three times a week, to walk through both floors of his firm.

"I talk to all of the men, even if it's just to ask them meaningless questions not at all related to work. I discuss sports, the weather, skiing—anything to let them know I exist and I'm available. Sure, it takes an hour out of every day, but it pays off. They all know me and trust me, and their work shows it."

I'm a minor executive in a large oil company, but I'm eager to climb the corporate ladder. I've noticed that at our staff meetings there is a lot of jockeying for position between the boss and the executives as well as among the executives themselves. Are there rules to all this, and could I profit by learning them?

You can learn a great deal from careful observation. People reveal a lot about themselves in meetings of this sort. The executive who gets too close to the boss's desk is usually declaring his allegiance. While the boss may approve and award him "brownie points," his fellow executives will be suspicious of his motives. They'll begin to think he's out to get them. Remember back in school how you felt about the teacher's pet who took the desk closest to the teacher?

However, if an executive positions himself away from or behind his teammates, he'll make them uneasy and damage the cohesiveness of the team. If he decides to stand while they sit, he makes the separation even more obvious.

Dr. Mortimer R. Feinberg of the City University of New York cited these examples of team interaction in a recent article and went on to note that while this jockeying for position takes place, the boss in turn will be reacting to his executives with a very subtle, but revealing, body language of his own.

He'll acknowledge the arrival of each employee with an abstracted glance, probably accompanied by a "quick minuscule smile." If the boss starts talking at once, he's making it clear that he's about to lecture his executives, not confer with them. The longer he talks, the more obvious it is that he's in control, and the more certain it is that any executive will hesitate to volunteer his own ideas. It takes a tough subordinate to be the first one to speak after a long harangue by the boss.

Watch your fellow executives during the meeting. They will usually avoid eye locks (catching and holding someone else's eye) while the boss is talking. Eye locks give the impression that they are plotting against him.

On the other hand, too long a smile at the boss, or too many head nods while he's talking, or too much leaning forward attentively all betray the "yes man" in the crowd to his fellow executives.

If yessing is to be done, and you cannot get up many rungs of the corporate ladder without it, it is most effective in a one-to-one situaton, not at a large meeting.

My friend Jim thinks he's a celebrity, but if he is, he's a very minor one. He plays with a rock group on weekends in a local bar. What gets me is that Jim always wears dark glasses. Since I've known him I've become aware that many famous people wear sunglasses all the time. Why do they do it?

Sometimes the celebrity who wears sunglasses does it as an affectation, and sometimes the glasses are used as a disguise. Occasionally, they're a genuine guard against too much sun. But aside from these, there is another valid reason why someone who is famous wants to hide his eyes.

The eyes are the parts of the body used most often in nonverbal communication. Hiding the eyes removes the possibility that a stranger might catch your eye and pull you into an unwanted conversation.

If someone does lock eyes with a celebrity and the celebrity ignores the signal, he runs the risk of offending a possible fan and harming his reputation. What he's saying is, "Yes, I see you but I'm not interested in talking to you."

For the ordinary person this is a perfectly acceptable way of discouraging inroads on his privacy. For the celebrity who must carefully watch his *image,* there is always the risk of appearing too self-important or too conceited to bother with the public.

Rather than risk this interpretation, the celebrity retires behind dark glasses and avoids the eye confrontation altogether. It's a much safer method.

There's something of a power struggle going on in our office, and Harold seems to have the edge. He's gotten it by anticipating so many of the boss's decisions that we're all beginning to wonder if he has extrasensory perception. When we put it to Harold directly, he just laughed and said, "Body language." But we've all been watching, and none of us notices anything obvious. Can there be slight gestures we don't see that Harold is able to use to his advantage?

Harold may be right. There are very slight gestures that we all use in body language—some so slight that it's hard to believe our eyes are quick enough to pick them up.

Scientists have photographed people in action and have had to play and replay the films dozens of times before they could pick up some of these seemingly insignificant gestures: a minute droop of an eyelid, a slight motion with a head or hand.

Amazingly enough, without being consciously aware of it, we all receive these tiny signals and understand them. The greater part of our body language communication, indeed, is on this subliminal level.

Now Harold may be picking these signals up from your boss and interpreting them to his own advantage in the power play you mentioned, but there is no reason to think the rest of you can't pick up the same signals—as a matter of fact, I'm sure you can.

It's likely, however, that Harold has other sources of information in anticipating the boss's directives and is just throwing the rest of you off the track by making you think he's relying just on body language.

Sam has been my business partner for ten years, and we manage to get along—except for one thing that bothers me. Sam has the most annoying handshake. When you shake hands with him, you always end up with only his fingers. What does this type of handshake mean? For that matter, how much can you tell about a person from his handshake?

A handshake is a very revealing body language signal, and it can give you some important clues to what the shakee really thinks of you. The odds are that Sam, who offers you only the fingers of his hand, doesn't like you too much, or else doesn't want to become too involved with you. Perhaps, since you're partners, this is a wise choice.

The person who shakes hands like a limp fish, offering you the entire hand but with "no bones" is probably ill at ease and unused to shaking hands. The chances are he doesn't like to be touched, and he submits to the handshake, but he does so feeling it's a necessary violation of his privacy. There is also a possibility that the limp handshaker has an inner arrogance that he wants to conceal.

On the other hand, the firm handshake gives an impression of quiet confidence. "I'm glad to meet you" is the unspoken message. Also: "I'm a no-nonsense person, competent and at ease." Unfortunately, the firm handshake is often a learned reflex and may reveal very little of the true man. Men are taught to shake firmly in this society—not too heavily, but not too lightly. The businessman learns this quickly, and his firm, pleasing handshake is usually training. But it is still the most acceptable shake.

The *macho* shake is superhard and firm, a test of strength that says, "I have the power to cause pain if I want to!" Far from betraying his inner strength, the man with the *macho* shake usually hides a basic insecurity and the need to prove himself with every meeting.

In class the other day I tried to tell my teacher that
I had been too ill to research a paper, but she caught
me out in the lie. She said I gave myself away with my
uneasy eye contact. I've been wondering ever since if
I could have been more convincing. Tell me, can you
really lie in body language?

A study to determine just this was the subject of a
doctoral thesis submitted to Stanford University by
a student, Mark Snyder. Mark set up what he called a
"self-monitoring" approach to discover whether our expressions are consistent. "We may put on a happy face
to cover our sadness, but do we also use a happy tone
of voice?" Mark wondered. Forgetting to be this consistent would spoil any attempt to lie with our bodies.

After his study was completed, Mark concluded that
the face is usually controlled, but the body is often
forgotten. He found that the people he interviewed and
tested could be categorized. There were two distinct
types: self-monitors, who are sensitive to the expressions
and messages sent out by others and who use these cues
to manage their own body language, and non-self-
monitors, who don't care about their own body language
and who pay no attention to the expressions of others.

People who are strong self-monitors are good at learning
what's socially right in new situations. They adapt well
and they can control their own body language and lie
rather successfully in body language.

Actors were the strongest self-monitors, the best liars.

Among the poorest self-monitors were ward patients in psychiatric hospitals.

Here are six of the true-false statements that helped Mark separate self-monitors from non-self-monitors:

(1) I can only argue for ideas I already believe.

(2) I guess I put on a show to impress or entertain people.

(3) I rarely need the advice of my friends to choose movies, books, or music.

(4) I'm not always the person I appear to be.

(5) At a party I let others keep the jokes and stories going.

(6) I may deceive people by being friendly when I really dislike them.

Altogether, there were twenty-five such statements in Mark Snyder's "lie-detector test." The testee was asked to answer them a honestly as he could.

Just as a sample, if you answered the above six questions this way—(1) false, (2) true, (3) false, (4) true, (5) false, and (6) true— then you rate high on the self-monitoring scale. You are probably a rather skilled liar in body language!

I'm a doctor in general practice, and the problems my patients bring me range from physical to emotional. It seems to me I've heard every frailty of human nature that there is. Usually I can listen in a nonjudgmental

way, but I find that if I've had any upsetting problem at home or in the hospital it becomes very difficult to deal with my patients. They seem to sense my inner tension. What body language giveaway clues am I projecting?

The very simple ones that betray your troubled feelings are probably found in your face. People who see themselves on television or film are frequently amazed at the tension and anxiety betrayed by their own faces. "Is that the way I look?" is usually their first response, and then, "But I tried so hard to cover my nervousness—or did I?"

When you see your patient after a trouble-filled day at home or in the hospital you project your own anxiety in dozens of ways—the tight eyebrows, the intent frown, the narrowed eyes and downcast mouth. All of these can give you away.

Not only your face but your body, too, can betray your true feelings. Slumped shoulders signal depression. Repetitive gestures—tapping your hand or foot—indicate impatience or nervousness. Tension is often betrayed by a clenched fist or rigid stance.

One doctor I spoke to about this problem pointed out that he had learned from his patients. The women hide their anxieties behind elaborate hairdos or dark glasses. The men shield their eyes or look away when they're anxious. The anxious patient often sits on the edge of his chair, he told me. "Or he'll lean on my desk. I watch them and search for the same betraying signs in myself.

Often I can catch my own anxiety in time to keep the patient from seeing it."

When this doctor spots an anxious patient, he advises him to sit back, drop his hands, and breathe slowly. "Even if it doesn't relax them, it makes them laugh and recognize that they *are* tense. I think that recognition is the first step in reducing tension."

I watched Henry Kissinger on television the other night, and I noticed that when he speaks he usually uses only one hand to gesture. What does this mean?

When a man unconsciously holds back on his body language gestures, limiting his motion to half his body or to only one arm, there is always the possibility that he is trying to hold back verbal information as well.

However, it is important to understand that a man must be judged in the total context of his personality and his cultural background. This means the culture he was born into and the one in which he spent his formative years, as well as the one he lives in as an adult.

Kissinger came to America in his teens, and his ethnic origin is Jewish-European, his immediate ancestors coming from Germany. Typically, according to scientists who have analyzed hand gestures, the body language gestures of Jews who come from this area tend to be "one-handed, choppy, staccato, and filled with energy."

Kissinger's body language then, apart from concealing anything, may simply reveal his own cultural background. It is interesting, in watching Kissinger, to see how limited his body language is in general. Even his smile hardly lifts one side of his mouth. This is unusual in a man whose cultural background would lead us to expect a much more vigorous body language.

What it all reveals is a great deal of careful control —something you would expect and desire in a man in such an important position.

Why do so many politicians move so awkwardly when they're on television? When I watch them, I begin to get uncomfortable, and I wish they'd stand still.

Perhaps you are right and many of them would convey a better image if they remained motionless during their speeches. Whenever they move awkwardly, you can give odds that they are trying to learn "proper" body language because some bright public relations man has convinced them that hand movements convey warmth and sincerity and can make them more popular with the voters.

What they often fail to realize is that hand motions are linked to culture and language. If you grow up in a culture that favors hand motions, the Italian culture, for example, then hand motions come naturally and seem natural to the person who watches you.

But if you grow up in one of the cultures that favor limited hand motions, such as the Swedish culture, and you decide to add such movements to your body language repertoire, there will be an inevitable period when using them seems forced and awkward.

Eventually, with practice and the proper critical analysis, you can learn a smooth body language delivery. Most politicians do. But a close observer always gets a feeling of unease, of something out of synch, when he watches a man raised in a culture with toned-down arm movements attempt to use his hands fluently.

It would be far better for a politician to be basically honest, and then let his body project that honesty unconsciously. He could then forget about *how* he was talking and concentrate on *what* he was talking about—but probably that wouldn't be politic.

Many years ago I had the good fortune to be present at an informal news conference with President Lyndon Johnson, and I heard him use the expression "press the flesh." What do you think he meant by this?

Johnson may have been using a political colloquialism for shaking hands, but it's more likely he was referring to his own very successful technique of handshaking. He not only grasped someone's hand, but also, with his other hand, grasped the arm above the elbow, thus making a double contact.

Johnson was well aware of how important body contact is in reassuring people and giving them an impression of warmth. The extra touch said, "I like you so much that I not only shake your hand but I touch your arm as well. I press your flesh."

This touching and breaking through the zone of privacy we all like to carry around with us can convey warmth and friendliness. Many politicians have learned that this extra touch is well worth the friends it makes. While Johnson may have been perfectly sincere in his gesture, in many politicians touching is a very calculated action. Touching the arm, the shoulder—even kissing babies—is something they learn early in campaigning. It's one way of getting close to the people.

New York City's former mayor John Lindsay attempted to get close by walking among crowds in his shirt-sleeves, going into troubled areas when riots threatened. His presence successfully cooled many hot city situations. He was there. He could be reached. Television and films showed that hundreds of young and old people reached out to touch him as he walked. The shirt-sleeve appearance was another public image gimmick—also successful. It said, "I'm like you, no jacket, an ordinary man."

There was a very limited number of people Mayor Lindsay or President Johnson could reach with actual body contact. What the gestures primarily accomplished was a public image of men very quick to shake hands and not afraid of touching. This image, they hoped, would send reassurance and comfort to the American public.

I watched a speech by our senator the other day, and when it was over I felt angry and betrayed. All the things he said so persuasively were just not true. I sometimes feel that politicians tell so many lies that I would like to give up in disgust and mistrust everything they say. Are there any clues in their body language to help me know when they are telling the truth and when they are lying?

There are many clues, but often they are difficult to read, and if the politician is skilled he may learn to control the clues and send a sincere and earnest message no matter what he's saying.

The only salvation the voter has is the fact that often subliminal clues are sent out, no matter how skillfully the politician controls his body. These clues are often too fleeting to notice consciously, but they have an unconscious influence on the watcher. You watch and distrust the speaker although you can't say exactly what it was that made you mistrust him.

Motion pictures slowed down considerably may give some clues, and so, for that matter, can still photographs. A national newspaper once took 20 rolls of still photos of Richard Nixon giving a State of the Union message, a total of 720 single shots. They keyed each photo to a transcript of his speech.

A body language authority was asked to look at the pictures to try to determine when the former President was being less than truthful.

More than ten clear-cut signs of "holding back" or contradiction were spotted, and then the photos were compared with the speech. All the holding back signs occurred at controversial points in the speech. The newspaper finally decided not to publish the story, but subsequent events have indicated that all ten photos were taken when Nixon was indeed being equivocal!

Another body language "betrayal" came when President Nixon gave a televised news conference during the Vietnam war. A reporter asked how long we would be in Cambodia—we had just gone in—and Nixon was very reassuring, very smooth in what he said and in his body language, as he assured the reporter and the nation via television that there was nothing to be alarmed about and this was only a temporary action with no fighting men involved.

A perceptive cameraman, however, focused the television camera on Nixon's fist, which was firmly clenched at his side, so firmly clenched that the knuckles were white! This tiny sign of tension was picked up and transmitted to the entire nation.

It is just these tiny betrayals that tell us when, even with the most carefully rehearsed body language, a politician may or may not be telling the truth. Every man has some weakness in bearing or expression that gives away his tension.

I know I'm very sensitive to other people, and I know this means I can read their body language better than the average person. But I'm also very good at summing up people and telling whether they're real or phony. Is this tied up with my being able to read body language? How can I use this talent to my advantage?

It probably is. A Harvard experiment showed that good body language readers were also good judges of people. They seem to be more capable of learning a great deal of information about their own behavior and the behavior of others.

By tuning into this knowledge, they can often come up with complex but integrated explanations about someone's character. Usually they don't know that they're doing it. That little computer in the brain ticks away and adds up and subtracts, and there you are—a judgment.

Another area sensitive body language readers do well in is predicting other people's behavior. Understanding a person's body language gives them the power to predict what that person will do—and so they can control a subordinate more easily, knowing intuitively what's on his mind; or they can anticipate the boss's wishes more easily, and be right far more often than the next person. This ability is a sort of natural wisdom, and may be as important as pure intelligence—or more important.

When I was a boy, my father always insisted that I shake hands with someone when I was introduced. I like doing it now, but I've always wondered how the custom started. What's the history of the handshake?

The handshake goes back to the days when men carried weapons and strangers were regarded with suspicion. Grasping another's hand guaranteed that neither of you had a concealed weapon in that hand. It was a gesture of peace. You were also giving someone your weapon hand to hold.

The firmness of your grip showed your strength and served as a warning as well. But there was something else to the act of shaking hands. The very contact, the act of touching, lent confidence. Today the element of touch in handshaking is perhaps the strongest part of the gesture. By the nature of your touch, you can signal disdain or liking or pleasure or a dozen other emotions.

I'm a teacher, and I've been having this running argument with my principal. He keeps suggesting that I go down among the students when I lecture, or at least that I stand in front of my desk. But I'm a bit nervous about teaching anyway, and I feel much more

comfortable behind my desk. What position gives a teacher the most control over what goes on in the classroom?

To sit or stand on a platform in front of a class or any audience puts you in a vulnerable position. You are exposed and open. To stand in front of a desk, or sit on a corner of it, is still being exposed, but not quite as much as facing the class with no desk at all. The desk, even behind you, helps dissipate your vulnerability.

To go down and stand among the students or to sit on one child's desk leaves you even more vulnerable, but—as your principal understands—it will also free you. You are no longer locked in by that desk and all it symbolizes.

For the students, doing away with the desk brings you closer to them. It takes one barrier away and makes learning more likely. You're less formidable, more reachable and, all in all, better able to teach. Try it. You may like it.

One word of warning: Don't go into the classroom and sit at one of the student's desks. This brings you too far down to their level and abolishes what status you may have as teacher. If you sit among the students, try perching on one of their desks to preserve the advantage of physical height and, with it, dominance.

Last week my class of nine-year-olds seemed very dull. There was absolutely no discussion, and I felt that I was talking to a blank wall. I wasn't feeling well, and I wondered if it was something I failed to do that turned my students off. Are there any gestures I can learn to draw out class discussion?

There are some obvious ones that usually work. You can signal with your cupped hands the way a traffic cop does when he wants the cars to come forward. It's an encouraging gesture, and the students often respond to it unconsciously. Do it with both hands at shoulder level, the palms facing your body and the fingers closing and opening. Do it briefly, as a stimulus, after you ask a question.

If you want a student to modify his comments, lean to one side while he's talking. Again, taking a tip from traffic control, a raised hand slows up or stops a student.

It's often a good idea to walk forward and touch a student when you're disagreeing with him. Putting a hand on his shoulder says, in effect, "I think you're wrong in what you're saying, but it doesn't mean I don't like you. My touch says I do."

The touch will also give the student some encouragement to get back into the discussion later on.

Recently, a young lady in one of the classes I teach gave me a particularly hard time. Not that she did anything wrong, but I just couldn't get her to pay attention and stop whispering to her neighbor. Is there some way I could have gotten her attention without embarrassing her by telling her to pay attention?

With this situation, you could try calling on the student sitting next to the inattentive young lady. If she still didn't come around, you could call on the student on the other side. In effect, you're slowly zeroing in on her and she's bound to sit up and take notice.

If you have a situation where one student is addressing the class and your problem student isn't listening, try moving toward the nonlistener, walking down to her, and, if necessary, actually sitting on the edge of her desk.

When you do this, your attention will be somewhere else, on the student reciting, but your body presence and body language is directed to the inattentive one. The odds are that the troublesome student will straighten up and start listening. It's hard for any student to ignore a teacher's close physical presence.

I teach a class in an adult education program, and often I have to fight their conversation for the first few minutes. Are there any subtle ways I can let them know I'm ready to start?

It's not subtle, but a loud "Let's start now!" is very effective. If you want something subtler, there are many little signals and tricks you can cultivate to announce that you are ready.

An instructor I know has a little ritual charade to announce the beginning of his lecture. He takes off his jacket and hangs it up very deliberately, then rolls up his shirtsleeves. This not only signals "I'm ready" but also "I'm going to work." Then he tells a student to close the door.

He finds these signals very effective. It's a slow start, but a definite one. By the time he's ready to begin, the class has quieted down.

He also ends his lecture behind his desk, and he gathers up his notes with his last few words, signaling that it's all over.

This same instructor has a few "fail-safe" signals to stop a long-winded student. He looks at the clock or takes off his watch. If these fail, he tells me, "I simply cough, then speak up and tell him he's talked long enough!"

I teach a class of college students, and I notice that some always sit in the same place—at the ends of the class. Is there any significance to this, or for that matter to where students sit in general?

There's a great deal of significance. The students who sit at either side are attempting to position themselves out of your line of sight. They reason that they are much less likely to make eye contact with you if they're seated there. They'll be less likely to be recognized and called on.

They may do this because they aren't completely involved in the course, or they may resent having to take it, be chronically unprepared, or suffer from any one of the dozens of possible reasons, including shyness, that would make them want to stay out of your area of attention.

Where a student chooses to sit in a classroom can tell you a great deal about him and his relationship to the teacher. Usually, if there are more seats than students and the students all have free choice, more of them will tend to cluster in the seats near the door. This may be because they feel a certain safety factor in being able to reach the door quickly or because they want to disassociate themselves from the class, or it may simply be that they do not want to cross the entire room to a chair. In each case, it is usually a function of how they relate to the teacher or the subject being taught.

As a rule, quiet students, those less likely to enter discussions, tend to sit at the edges of the classroom. Often, those who will recite sit in the back, down the center of the class, and along the front.

Traditionally, the "good" students will choose the front seats. Those who chose the back row, as a rule, are suspicious of the class or the teacher—even though they may contribute.

The ones who sit closest to the back door, if there is a front and a back entrance, are those not fully into the class, not fully convinced of its importance and benefits.

In most cass, a student will take one seat and come back to that same seat for each succeeding lecture, as if a strong sense of territory made that his domain. But if, during the course of the class, his attitude toward teacher and students changes, he will often shift his seat.

With all of these factors in mind, the canny teacher can anticipate student behavior by noting not only where each student chooses to sit at the beginning of the term, but also where he moves to during the term.

A group of teachers in our high school got into an argument recently about the advantages and disadvantages of being autocratic. A few teachers felt that a democratic approach was better, but we couldn't reach a consensus. In terms of body language, which do you think is better?

I'm not sure what you mean by "in terms of body language." If you mean, which group of teachers is better at reading the students' body language, then the answer is those using the democratic approach.

A test devised at Harvard University attempted to discover the differences between the autocratic and the democratic approach in the classroom. It concluded that the democratic teachers were more sensitive to nonverbal cues.

But it is difficult to tell which came first. Were those teachers who were more sensitive to students' feelings and body language more likely to be democratic, or did democracy encourage such sensitivity to develop?

For that matter, does autocratic behavior have the reverse effect by making teachers less sensitive to others, or do the less sensitive teachers tend to be autocratic?

I'm a teacher, and one of the problems I face is understanding my students' reactions. The other day I spent half an hour teaching a theorem, but when I asked the students to explain it, no one had understood. Is there some way I could read their body language to know when they were getting the point or when they weren't?

Often the wrong kind of body language sets a barrier between students and teacher. Your facial expression, tone of voice, and gestures may be telling your students things about you that you'd rather they didn't know— are you tense, rigid in your views, punitive? All these things and more are revealed in your face and movements.

In teaching, there is a constant feedback from teacher to student and student to teacher. It takes very little to convince your students that you're critical of them or ridiculing them. You can never assume that they understand you or are listening to you unless the proper feedback tells you so.

How can you be aware of the proper feedback? Keep eye contact. Constantly sweep the room with your eyes and don't concentrate only on that bright face in the front row. Watch for the frown, the glazed look, the preoccupied expression—these are the students who aren't getting your message.

On the other hand, become aware of the nodding head, a body language statement that says "Yes. I understand. I agree. I'm with you." If you fail to get this signal, then the odds are you haven't made your point. Don't go on. Find the weak spot and correct it.

I've noticed a funny thing in my fifth-grade class this term. I don't know if they're brighter than any classes I've had before, but for some reason I like all the students, and I'm surprised to find that they're all doing better than my other classes did. Am I communicating something to them with my body language? I know that my teaching method is the same as it's always been.

There are many ways in which a teacher can communicate her expectations to her class: her tone of voice, the expression on her face, touching the students, her posture.

A researcher in this field found that teachers with a positive attitude toward their students—that is, teachers who expected the best and usually got it—often touched the students and came close to them. They tended to lean forward when they taught, held eye contact, gesticulated more than most teachers and moved their heads, nodding more frequently and smiling more often. Their faces, too, were more animated and expressive.

What it adds up to is that these teachers were more

communicative on a nonverbal level. They sent out messages constantly, and these messages were interpreted by the students as "I have faith in you. You'll do well!"

Studies have shown that teachers get more out of students they think are gifted, and they communicate through body language more intensely with those students. The strange thing that these studies show is that the children need not be particularly gifted *as long as the teacher thinks they are.* On an unconscious level, her body language encourages and brings out the best in them.

I'm an avid watcher of television talk shows, and I'm struck by the different body language of the hosts. I've noticed, for example, that while Merv Griffin and Mike Douglas seem compelled to touch their guests, Johnny Carson is always separated from them by his desk. What do the hosts gain from these different positions?

The body language of talk show hosts reflects their techniques. Mike Douglas will hang on his guest's words, nod feelingly with every statement, clutch at an arm or shoulder, and project to the audience the message that he is intensely interested in everything his guest has to say and, by golly, the audience should be interested too!

Merv Griffin is even more intrigued by his guests, round-eyed and overly intense and delighted to be there with them—or at least this is what his body says. The delight spills over, making it hard for any audience not to enjoy him and his guest.

The body language of both serves the same purpose a laugh track serves in a situation comedy. The laugh track programs the viewer and tells him what's funny and when to laugh. The talk show host's body language tells the viewer not only what's funny, but who to like, who to enjoy, when to be fascinated, and when to be impressed, and, of course, when to have a good time.

Carson plays a different role. Most of his guests pay homage to him. Griffin and Douglas pay homage to the guests. To make the difference clear, Carson puts himself behind a desk, removing himself physically from his guests and also from his TV audience. He becomes someone apart, someone to woo. And, in contrast to the other talk show hosts, Carson is tougher and harder on his guests, more cynical and sardonic.

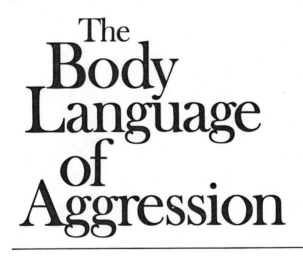

The
Body
Language
of
Aggression

I often go to a singles bar for fun and companionship, and I've wondered about the crowding that goes on there. I like my privacy, and ordinarily I can't stand people pushing in on me, but in bars I never seem to mind. Why is that?

We all carry bubbles of privacy around with us, much the way astronauts carry space helmets. But our privacy bubbles are invisible, and their size depends on our individual needs. They are also related to our culture. Some people, especially those from northern countries, prefer two feet of clear space all around them. They are most comfortable when they talk to others at this distance. People from other cultures, the Arabs for example, are happier with small privacy bubbles; six inches of space is enough.

But all these requirements have their exceptions. There are situations where bubbles of space can merge pleasantly. When two people are in love, it's natural and desirable to cut into each other's space, to come closer than your privacy bubble normally dictates. A mother can intrude on her child's space without discomfort. A pair of workers, a teacher and student, a doctor and patient may all, under certain circumstances, intrude on each other's space without any problem.

The same intrusion is acceptable in a crowded bar, provided we wish to be there and enjoy the bar scene. If we don't like bars, then we resent the crowding that occurs. If we like the bar scene as you do, then we accept the special intrusions as not only permissible but actually desirable.

Unfortunately, alcohol often distorts our privacy bubbles, and our needs for private space may change once we've had a few drinks. Our bubbles may melt away altogether, or they may get larger and harder so that we resent any intrusion at all. This is one reason that violence often erupts in bars. Some people develop exaggerated bubbles of privacy, and when others are crowded up against them they take it as an act of aggression.

Recently, at a business conference with another firm, my boss lit a cigar. He is an occasional smoker, but there was something peculiar about the way he held his cigar at that meeting and about the way he gestured with it. Is this use of a cigar a body language gesture, and if so, what does it mean?

To some extent a cigar is an extension of a man's own body. It is often used to emphasize his unconscious feelings during a major business conference. It may be held high in an upward tilt when the smoker feels that he is in a strong, dominant position.

A cigar is often used as a weapon of aggression in a face-to-face confrontation. While it is usually considered impolite to point, the cigar smoker can use his cigar in lieu of a pointer, or he may use it to zero in on another man. The longer the cigar, the more effective this tactic.

We all have personal zones of privacy in which we feel comfortable and safe. Intrusion by someone else into these zones makes us feel uneasy. By leaning across a conference table and using the cigar as an extension of his hand to break into another's zone, the cigar-smoking executive can put someone else at a disadvantage. The cigar becomes a tool of aggressive threat.

My husband, Erick, is a good provider, and I love him dearly. We've been married for twenty years and have two teen-age children. The trouble is, there's one

thing about Erick that drives the whole family crazy.
He never lets any of us finish what we have to say.
He interrupts whenever I begin to talk. Sometimes he
finishes what we begin, but more often his interruptions
have nothing to do with what we're saying. Are we
all too slow for Erick, or is something else wrong?

It may be that Erick has never learned to read the
proper turn-taking signals needed to carry on a two-way
conversation. We use these signals without being aware
that we're doing so, and we read them automatically.
When we finish a sentence, we lower the pitch of our
voice. When we ask a question, we raise it. If we mean
to keep talking, we hold the pitch level. We also raise,
lower, and keep level our head, eyes, eyebrows, and
hands to match our voice pitch.

These are the basic signs of turn-taking. If, for some
reason, Erick doesn't know them, he will blunder along
in his conversation, always interrupting at the wrong
time and often neglecting to pick up the proper cue to
tell him when to speak.

If you noticed long pauses in your talks with Erick, as
well as the interruptions you report, you might assume that
he was ignorant of the signals.

However, since you notice only interruptions, the problem may be something else. Interrupting in this way is
often a sign of aggression. The one who does it is
usually trying to dominate the other people or the situation, although he may not be aware of what he's doing.

To return this treatment in kind just makes for a struggle for dominance that can turn into a quarrel. To submit is wrong, too, because it eventually arouses your own hostility and anger.

It is important for you and your children to stick up for your own rights and tell Erick each time he interrupts, "I want to finish my sentence."

Sometimes it's a good idea to do this publicly or socially. What he can bluff through in his own family, he may think twice about with other people. Of course, you take the risk of Erick's annoyance or anger. That could be unpleasant. But you also have the chance that he will become aware of what he does and try to change. The results may be worth the risk.

I live in a neighborhood that isn't too safe, and on my way to the bus stop, going to or coming home from work, I have to go down some unpleasant streets. I often worry about the men I pass. Usually I avoid looking at them because I'm afraid that eye contact may be an invitation to the potential mugger. Is this true, or could I anger them by doing this?

Avoiding the eyes of a potential mugger by walking briskly and looking past him suggests that you have a definite goal. This makes you a slightly less attractive target. But, on the other hand, eye contact implies recognition, and recognition is the mugger's enemy. He likes to work in stealth and anonymity. He wants to single you out, but he doesn't want you to single him out.

I can't advise you either way. There are advantages and disadvantages to both approaches. By making eye contact, you give him the right to approach you, but you also warn him off.

Above all, the average mugger doesn't want trouble. He's looking for an easy victim, preferably a drunk or an older person or a lone woman. He'll avoid anyone who's too big or too strong or who projects confidence.

How do you project confidence and strength? Well, in body language, the primary signal is in the walk. Walk with assurance; erect and with your shoulders back. If you're a man, you could swagger. According to a number of actors, a swagger means a slight roll to the shoulders— an athlete's walk. Flex your arms and let your feet hit solidly. Keep your hips parallel to the ground.

Usually a woman can't project this kind of physical confidence, and she shouldn't try. But she can walk briskly and purposefully and, if possible, keep away from dangerous streets. If, as in your case, you must travel such streets, the police have given some definite rules to follow.

When you walk a deserted street at night, walk briskly and keep alert. In body language, you will send out a message of "I know where I'm going. I'm familiar with this neighborhood, and my familiarity may be dangerous to you if you try to mug me. I'm at home here."

The police warn against ambling, window-shopping, or betraying uncertainty by hesitating and looking around.

Like a predator in the jungle, the mugger looks for an easy target: the weak, the unsure, the uncertain. You can discourage him by sending out a body language signal of strength and confidence.

However, the police also warn against any foolhardy action. If you think a mugger is following you, don't hesitate to yell. Forget about being embarrassed, and make plenty of noise. It is far better to make a mistake by being overcautious than to make a mistake by being foolishly brave.

I was walking down the street the other day, when a panhandler came toward me. I'll admit I stared because he looked as if he had been sleeping in his clothes for a month. There were other people on the street, but he singled me out and started following me, asking for money. I kept shaking my head and walking faster, and luckily there was an officer at the corner and the man fell back and approached someone else. How can I discourage an incident like that?

By saying no as you did. You can also discourage a panhandler in body language by avoiding eye contact. You say you stared, and this made eye contact. Once you meet his eye, you acknowledge his presence and you must go through the whole refusal bit unless you want to give him some change.

Catching anyone's eye, even a panhandler's, means that

you recognize him as a fellow human being. You establish a bond of communication and make it easier for him to approach you. Avoid his eye and you deny his presence, making him into a nonperson.

On the street one day, I stood and watched a blind beggar with his dog stand in front of a department store and beg for change. I found it fascinating to note that most of the people who approached him and didn't want to give him anything avoided his eyes, even though he was blind. They were so aware of the importance of eye contact as a recognition signal that they automatically refused it to a blind man!

The other day I got into the elevator in my office building—it's automatic—and another man got on just as the doors closed. There was something so threatening about him, the way he moved, that I jabbed the button for the second floor, got off, and took another elevator up. I don't know if this guy was a businessman or a mugger, but are there any body language giveaways that could help me tell the difference? How can I avoid dangerous situations in an elevator?

First, you should obey the obvious rules of safety when you are riding an unattended elevator. If you're a woman and there's only one man in the elevator, don't get on. Wait for the next one. Remember—elevators are like lovers. If you miss one, another will always be along!

If a man pushes in before the doors close and you are alone with him, push out. When you enter, stay near the controls so you can push the nearest floor and the alarm if anyone threatens you.

As for spotting a dangerous fellow rider, remember that a man who is going to attack you in an elevator—whether you're a man or woman—is acting a role. He won't be likely to betray himself with a suspicious look. You have to rely on your gut reaction. If you feel any uneasiness, don't take a chance. Get out. Better offend someone by playing safe than take a chance to spare their feelings.

But if you are careless and find yourself in an elevator with another passenger who turns out to be dangerous, the one thing you can do is try to make "contact" and disarm his aggression. The trick is to make him see you as a human being rather than a victim. For example, catch his eye, smile, and ask him what time it is. Throw him off balance by moving in in an overly friendly fashion.

A friend of mine found himself in just this situation recently. Paul had entered an elevator in a large office building, and just before the doors closed a husky, rough-looking man pushed in. He and Paul were alone in the elevator.

The way Paul tells it, it was the other's manner that alerted him. "There was something about the way he moved and looked at me. I felt threatened, and I just knew I was in for trouble."

"What did you do?"

"I moved in fast before he could collect himself. I

began talking to him. I said, 'Hey, I've got an appointment upstairs in five minutes. I hope I'm not late. Have
you got the right time?'

"Before he could answer, I moved close to him and
he stepped back, automatically looking at his watch. I
knew I had only a minute before I reached my floor, but
a minute can be forever. If he was a mugger, he'd have to
move fast, and I had put him off stride. He looked kind of
startled, like maybe he was assessing the whole thing.
Did he have enough time?

"While he was trying to decide, I was at him with
another question. Had he noticed the two cops on the
ground floor? Was anything going on in the building?
Before he could answer, we were at my floor and I scooted
out. Now maybe he wasn't a mugger, but then again,
maybe he was. I couldn't take a chance. Let him think I
was a kook. It was worth it."

In terms of body language, what Paul had done was to
refuse to act the role of a victim. He had acted aggressively, on a verbal and nonverbal level, and it was a tight
enough situation—dictated by the few minutes before his
floor came—for it to work.

I walked into a new church last Sunday, and during
the services one of the men stared at me a number of
times. Each time he must have looked at me for over
a minute. I found myself growing angry out of all

proportion to his curiosity, and I can't understand why
I reacted that way. Can you explain why a simple
stare annoyed me so?

We all feel that a direct, steady stare from a stranger is
either an insult or a threat. It violates society's *moral looking time,* a time that varies from situation to situation.
In a public place like a church, the moral looking time is
relatively short. If someone looks at us in church for too
long a period, we may react as you did, feel uneasy,
threatened, and then angry.

This reaction to extended stares is very prevalent among
animals. Monkeys and gorillas become angered and excited when other animals or men stare directly at them.
They respond with growls and threatening gestures. A
remnant of this instinctive fear in men is our myth about
the evil eye, the magic power of too steady a stare.

In the incident you describe, the other man may simply
have been curious about a visitor to his church, but never-
theless he was breaking the unwritten code about how
long one can stare at another in a public place. You
interpreted his curiosity as a threat or rudeness. Staring
back with a friendly smile is a traditional way of ending
this rudeness.

My Uncle Fred lives with us, and he drinks very
heavily—in fact Uncle Fred's really a lush! Mom says
that the liquor has dulled his brain. Of course, none
of us would come right out and tell him he's an alcoholic

—but I notice that he doesn't even seem to read the obvious disapproving body language signals we send him. Why not? Is he just too aggressive about his right to drink to care what we think?

An interesting fact has come to light through studies with alcoholics.

Researchers have found that whenever a situation gets too complex, psychiatric and alcoholic patients run into trouble reading the body language of other people. They can read the simple signs, but not the complicated ones. The trouble seems to be that neither psychiatric patients nor alcoholics can handle too much information.

They can only observe a limited number of signals, and they only send out a limited number. The psychiatric patients are probably too involved with their own separate realities. Their worlds are limited by their illness.

The alcoholic patients, however, simply do not have the available nervous pathways to handle the nonverbal communication. Alcohol anesthetizes part of the brain and nervous system.

Your mother, probably reacting in sheer disgust to Uncle Fred, has put her finger on the problem. If he takes in enough alcohol, it may well dull Uncle Fred's brain.

My brother-in-law, Howard, is very peculiar about people coming close to him. He gets very angry and upset, sometimes violent. Last week, Howard came home with a black eye after a fight in a bar. According to him, someone else was "crowding him," but the bartender told my husband that no one was really that close to him. Why does Howard act this way? Is it normal?

It doesn't sound normal, but it does happen. All of us have a sense of territory, a space around ourselves that we don't like others to encroach on. Many of us feel an undercurrent of violence when we are crowded in a bus or subway. We feel threatened and uneasy.

Most people are uncomfortable with this feeling even when it can't be avoided. They resent being shoved around. When it happens, they feel their entire body tense up. Women particularly often report they feel "violated" by such crowding.

When circumstances prevent us from keeping a comfortable distance from others, we become annoyed—not with ourselves or with the situation that causes the crowding, but with the other people involved. We may even feel that they are going to assault us.

Most of us manage to keep these feelings under control and in proportion, but there are a few people, like your brother-in-law, Howard, who can't control their annoyance, and any crowding at all makes them angry and even violent. A bar, of course, is often a crowded place and may exaggerate your brother-in-law's sensitivity. After a while, most patrons learn to keep their distance from someone like Howard.

Prison studies by Dr. Augustus F. Kinzel showed that

many of the men who errupted into violent behavior for no apparant reason actually thought that they were protecting their privacy zones from people who intruded. The only trouble was, their privacy zones were four times as large as the zones of nonviolent prisoners.

The anxiety felt by these violence-prone men when other prisoners came close to them has been labeled "intrusion panic" by Dr. Kinzel, and he says it's not very different from the panic that many babies feel when strangers come too close.

I was out driving with my boyfriend, Gary, and another car cut us off. Maybe the driver didn't see us, or maybe he was just being "cute." I know that if I was driving I would simply have moved out of his way. Who needs those kinds of games? But Gary went ape! What on earth makes some people so upset about another car cutting them off or tailgating them?

One probability is that Gary has problems with his own sense of masculinity. Cutting him off like that is a *macho* challenge, and many men will feel they have to respond and "get" the other fellow. The man who is most comfortable with his own maleness doesn't need such games to reassure himself. Check out Gary's attitude toward other men—and toward you. Is he always out to prove himself? Does he treat you as an equal—or as the "little woman," a delicate creature to be protected?

Of course, there is another possibility. Going "ape" on Gary's part may be intrusion panic, another wrinkle in the violation of personal space. Most drivers know where the limits of their cars are without having to check them out. The automobile becomes an extension of their body. If Gary has an exaggerated sense of privacy, he may become very uncomfortable when someone comes too close.

It's possible that he carries this exaggerated need for privacy over into his driving. What you may consider an acceptable distance becomes an intrusion to him and he may overreact. Unfortunately, this can lead to sudden death on the highway!

The other day I was on a very crowded bus, and I found that when I got off I was filled with anger. Thinking back, I realize that I often react this way. For hours afterward I had pains in my back and shoulders. Someone suggested that this happens because I'm too close to people to use body language. Is this the real reason?

Probably not. Most people, when forced into a crowded situation as you were in the bus, tense up. They feel, quite correctly, that their privacy is being invaded, violated, though often they are not aware of the reason for these feelings.

A group of people in a big-city subway during rush hour who were questioned by a social scientist all said they felt uncomfortable, and some had very strong terrors about being robbed or molested. Some kept their bodies tense, their muscles ready for any danger.

This constant tension during the crush of the ride is probably responsible for the pain you feel in your back and shoulders. Even after the ride is over, these muscles remain tense and in spasm.

The anger you feel comes from the invasion of your own ego, the sense of being assaulted and "pushed around." You become angry with everyone around you, and often, because you can't express the anger, it turns inward and shows up as a bewildering headache.

Sometimes it explodes outward, and fierce arguments spring up on crowded subways, buses, or trains, arguments out of all proportion to what has happened.

I teach a class of high school students, and I'm rather new at it and uncertain of myself. My students seem aware of this. How can I be a more assertive teacher? Is there some way of using body language to overcome my diffidence?

Absolutely. The surer you are in your movements and gestures, the more capable and assertive you will appear. Eventually, there should be a feedback in operation, and your forced assurance will become true assurance.

Come out from behind the protective desk and face your class. Different positions in front of the students can not only transmit confidence but can also break up the monotony of a teaching session.

If something is going on in class, some process of discussion among the students themselves, and you want to remove yourself from it, try leaning against the wall. Try to avoid pacing from side to side while you lecture. If you must move, try walking toward the students, even down among them as you talk.

To emphasize a point, walk forward. To minimize it or to reduce tension, draw back. Moving toward the class not only emphasizes things, but also increases the tension—something you will occasionally want to do if you wish to project aggression.

Teaching from the center of the class, usually on one of the desks, is a good strategy. It brings you closer to the students—but don't sit down in the student's chair. This lowers you to their level, and it is better for you to stay higher than your students, spatially. Being higher than they are gives you a certain aggressive dominance, something you evidently need.

My girfriend says I'm a lousy listener because I'm too restless. But I do listen, and I don't do anything as aggressive as interrupting the other talker, something she's always doing. Still, I must be doing something wrong. What makes a "good listener"?

Probably you are sending a contradictory message with your body as you listen with your mind. It takes more than verbal silence to be a good listener. There must also be body silence and body attention, body agreement and body disagreement. All these parts of body language tell the other person that you are tuned into what he's saying —or at least that you are trying to tune in.

Basically, the body language listening message that says "I am receptive" is stillness. Excessive movement, such as foot jiggling, tapping with the fingers or hand, or shifting your posture, all convey boredom and a desire to get it over with. It's difficult to talk to someone who sends this type of body message. You may not think you are aggressive, but you do send an aggressive message: "Shut up already and let me talk!"

A positive way of listening with your body is to adopt synchrony, a mirror image of the person talking, or a duplication of his posture. Copy his position as much as you possibly can, and imitate his hand arrangement, but do it subtly!

On an unconscious level, this signals "I agree with you," and it encourages him to keep talking. It assures him that you are listening. If you are in disagreement with what he says, your body should go out of synchrony—but you should still avoid nervous movements, turning your head aside and losing eye contact.

My husband always hunches forward with his shoulders stooped. He's a very hard worker and always has been, and now he's doing very well. True, he's not a very

aggressive man, but his posture makes him look as if
he's carrying the weight of the world on his
shoulders. What causes such stooping?

In your husband's case, you may have hit on the correct
answer with your description. He may just feel the
"weight of the world" on his shoulders. You describe him
as a hard worker, and, although he's successful now, if it's
been difficult for him to make it, he may have always felt
the weight of financial insecurity.

There is a feedback factor between a person's body
and self-esteem. If we feel aggressive and strong, we walk
with assurance and stand tall. If we are overwhelmed by
life, our posture reflects that, too. But very often, by
changing our posture, we can change our inner feelings.

If your husband could learn to walk without stooping,
to take some pride in his body, he might be able to trans-
late that pride to his inner self and become more aggressive, more sure of himself, less bowed down by life. If his
stooped posture no longer reflects his true feelings, he can
change it if he exerts enough effort. This, however, is only
possible if his "hard work" has succeeded in getting him
ahead in his job or business.

Stooping in men can also be a result of growing too tall
too soon. When a teen-ager is a head above his friends, he
often feels awkward and foolish. He will begin to com-
pensate by stooping to be less conspicuous, and eventually
the stoop becomes a normal posture.

Men hold no option on stooping. Women can also bow

beneath financial or family pressures. Some young girls will aquire stooped postures as their breasts begin to develop and they hunch forward to hide them. In the postadolescent years, pride in their bodies may straighten out both men and women stoopers—but unfortunately in many people the habit becomes too ingrained to break.

Our youngest child, Ellen, is very fearful and seems to have almost no aggressive instincts. In fact, the only stranger she lets come close to her is our next-door neighbor. From the moment she first saw him, she just smiled and reached out her hand to him. His wife says everyone likes her husband. It's his body language. But I can't figure out why. He's short and sort of funny-looking, with a big, bald head. The kids call him "Elmer Fudd." Can his body language really soothe Ellen?

I doubt if your neighbor's body language has anything to do with soothing Ellen, but his body may. I think you've hit on a very fascinating example of an innate releasing mechanism in human beings.

Experiments have shown that babies can react in different ways to things they have never experienced before —indicating some sort of built-in mechanism, a form of programming. If a shape comes toward a very young baby and expands evenly—indicating it will touch her— she will try to avoid it by turning aside. If it expands unevenly—indicating that it will miss her—she will accept it without flinching.

The baby, however, has no knowledge of what these shapes are. The shape itself and the manner in which it expands triggers the baby's response. In general, shapes can trigger responses. For example, we are programmed to become soft and sentimental when we see the shape of a human baby. Certain things about the baby's shape strike us as *cuddly*.

What is a cuddly baby? According to animal behaviorist Konrad Lorenz, a high forehead and in proportion to it, a small face, relatively large eyes, a small mouth, chubby cheeks, a large head in proportion to the body, and a chubby body shape are all attributes of "cuddliness."

Seeing all or any of these things gives us a feeling of protection and warmth. They not only release our nurturing instinct but they also dissipate any aggression we have and suppress our fears.

We don't need Konrad Lorenz to tell us this. Our doll manufacturers are well aware of it. Dolls are made in just this way: big heads, prominent foreheads, and all the rest. We label them "cute," and our children are immediately taken with them. A scientist would say they release the mothering instinct in the child. They overcome the fear instinct.

Cartoonists and animators are also aware of this, and Walt Disney has designed his "cute" characters with these attributes in mind. Bambi, the playful little satyrs in

Fantasia, the centaurs, and all his little animals are designed to evoke the protective response.

In the Bugs Bunny cartoons, pathetic little Elmer Fudd
is a classic example of a drawing designed to make us
smile with sympathy. He has all the attributes that make
for the "cuddly" look.

Your neighbor, whom the children have nicknamed
Elmer Fudd, must also have the "Cuddly" quality—as you
describe him. Undoubtedly, his appearance, funny to
you, is soothing, cute, and cuddly to Ellen. He releases
her protective instincts and allays her fears.

**Sue and I have been going together for over a year,
and I very much want to marry her. The trouble is, she
keeps saying no. When I finally pinned her down, she
said my style was just too aggressive. Sue is a very
mild person, and maybe we wouldn't get along living
together, but I love her enough to change. Can you
tell me what body language changes would help me
be more passive?**

The fact that you want to change for Sue is a very hopeful
sign. If you were truly aggressive through and through,
you would feel that Sue was wrong and she should
change, that you were fine as you are. Perhaps you've
gotten other reports about yourself from your other friends
and you realize that you are too aggressive.

I think, though, that you make an error in posing a

passive attitude as the answer. A certain amount of aggression is a useful commodity—especially if it's handled properly. It may well be that Sue could use more as you use less.

An even more productive solution is to examine three different styles of behavior instead of just passive and aggressive. Call the first of the three *aggressive,* the last *nonassertive.* This leaves a middle state: *assertive.* You can be assertive without being aggressive.

Assertiveness depends to a big extent on what you think of yourself. Are you worth something? If you are, you can stand up for yourself without being so aggressive that you intimidate the other person. Sue may not want an aggressive man, but she surely wants a man aware of his own worth and ready to speak out for it without overwhelming others.

In terms of communication and body language, the aggressive man is often too loud in his tone of voice. He tends to glare at people instead of looking at them, and, when he does look, he often looks too long, too intently. His gestures are apt to be angry. He may shake his fist or stamp his foot too often. He'll barge into things, a room, or a conversation.

To avoid being hurt himself, he'll hurt others, override others, blame them for things that go wrong, and be generally overbearing. It's not a pretty picture, and, if this is the way you act, you can understand why Sue would hesitate to commit herself to marriage.

On the other hand, the passive—or nonassertive—person

plays on the aggressive person's traits. He is hesitant in speech and manner, enters a room or a conversation only when bidden, and uses a diffident eye contact. He looks away, or down, and he'll even turn his body or head away when he's talking to you. His gestures are vague and nervous, and he smiles too much, an apologetic sort of smile.

In conversation, he agrees too much with others, avoids troublesome issues, and often speaks in a tone so low you can't hear him. He lets himself be hurt rather than hurt anyone else, and he avoids direct eye contact as he avoids direct confrontation.

It's not likely that you want to become like that, even for Sue—that is, if you ever could. An aggressive tiger cannot easily change his stripes. It would be far better to strive for the middle state: *assertiveness.*

The assertive man speaks in a moderate range and maintains good eye contact, but breaks it when it becomes uncomfortable. He faces up to others physically, leans toward the person he's talking to, holds his head erect, and doesn't slump during a conversation. He gestures with his hands and arms in a relaxed way, smiles in the right places, and avoids a tense, tight look around the mouth. Why? Because he's neither tense nor tight.

His tone of voice is level but clear, and he speaks easily without the constant pause-fillers, the "uhs" and "you knows" and "I means" and all the rest.

He values his own opinions as much as he values those of others, and he tries to avoid hurting or offending others as much as he avoids allowing himself to be hurt or offended.

This is the goal I think you would be wise to aim for, and it's also the goal you should encourage Sue to attempt. When two people have this type of assertiveness, they can live together comfortably.

During business meetings at our firm, I've noticed that when my boss gets very angry he throws his glasses down on the table. This gesture upsets me and the rest of the executives in our outfit. It's not just because the glasses might shatter, but something about the action itself makes me very uneasy. What is the meaning of this gesture?

The meaning is just what you said—that your boss is very angry. Throwing down a pair of glasses is very much like stamping your foot or slamming your fist against a table. It expresses anger and hostility.

Eyeglasses have a curious symbolism in body language. For one thing, they fit so well into the "Freudian pun." When you don't see eye to eye with someone, you will often remove your glasses while you're talking. It's a subtle, unconscious way of getting the message across.

However, this assumes that the person wears glasses because he is nearsighted. A farsighted person will remove glasses in order to see more clearly, and the removal will have an entirely different meaning.

A Manhattan optician, Dr. Alfred P. Poll, has been

observing the things people do with their glasses, and he has drawn some interesting insights. According to Poll, the executive who removes his glasses in a meeting and folds them into his case may be signaling that the meeting is over. The boss who shakes his glasses instead of his finger at an erring subordinate is tempering his rebuke. It would be stronger to use the finger alone.

Boredom, Poll feels, is signaled by folding and unfolding glasses, just as someone without glasses signals boredom with a small, repetitive act, such as doodling with a pencil or tapping the fingers. Poll goes on: Bending the temple bar reveals agitation; touching both temple tips together is tension or stress; chewing on the plastic temple end is nervousness.

Pushing the glasses up on the forehead, according to Poll, is a sign of honesty, but pushing them down the nose so that you can look over them is equal to saying, "You're putting me on."

Are all of these interpretations correct? Possibly. What is certain is that anything you hold—a pencil, a cigar, a pair of glasses—is an extension of your hand in body language terms. The meaning of the gesture you make with the held object is the same meaning you would give your empty hand, but exaggerated. The object makes the hand a little more than a hand, but no different.

I run a men's clothing store. I've always been aggressive in my selling techniques—and I've always

done well. Lately, I've been offered a good rental in a
new shopping plaza. I'm sure the plaza concept is
a good one, but what bothers me is that the location
offered to me is below street level. Is there anything
in the science of body language that would help
me make a decision about this?

A good part of the study of body language concerns itself
with how people handle space. We use space and react to
others' use of space in very determined ways. The size of
a store, the location of a store, and the layout of a store
all signal certain things to the prospective customer.

A recent study by two social scientists, Boris Pushkarev
and Jeffry M. Zupan, may hold the answer to your problem
on store location. The study, published by the Massa-
chusets Institute of Technology Press under the title
Urban Space for Pedestrians, discusses shopping plazas
in relation to sidewalks and pedestrians.

Most plazas, the study concludes, discourage pedestrian
use because they are above or below street level. This
should give you a clue to evaluating the location you're
considering. According to the MIT study, it just wouldn't
be as popular as a store at street level. To go up and down
stairs is enough of a deterrent to overcome the impulsive
buying that every shopkeeper relies on. You characterize
yourself as an aggressive seller, but your aggressiveness
would be of little use without the facilities for pulling in
the customers.

The study also notes that blocks with wide sidewalks

will attract more walkers. This might be another consideration when you do look for a location.

I'm the vice-president of the bank in a relatively small town, and I have a real problem—friendliness. Like last week, old Mr. Kelsoe came in, and when I finished his business, he just sat and sat forever! He's a good customer, but a little touchy—lonely, too—and he likes to talk. Is there some assertive body language I could use to let him know I have to get on with my work?

Of course, the best way to handle Mr. Kelsoe would be to smile after you've given him the amount of time you can spare and simply say, "I'd like to keep talking, but I have a load of work I must do." However, I assume that such a direct approach would upset him and that you're looking for a subtler way to ease him out.

You can start with some "finishing up" gestures: closing your desk drawer, pushing the papers on your desk together, and lining up your pens and pencils, rather definitely putting all your things aside. This says, "We're through now" and if your Mr. Kelsoe can pick up body language cues he'll begin to make going noises.

If he doesn't react to "finishing up" signals, you can offer him the next body language cue: move toward the edge of your seat and lean forward. This is a gentle body language "push," and most people, even if they don't react to the "finishing up" gestures, will react to this—at least by moving forward in their seat.

If, however, this still doesn't work, you can stand up. Pick a time while you're still talking to do it. It takes the sting away, but it still says, "We're finished now. I'll walk you to the door."

There are very few people who will ignore this signal. Some may take a minute or two to react, but they'll usually stand up too after a moment. If Mr. Kelsoe is one of the rare ones who remains sitting, then you have to take the last step of all. Still talking, start for the door. Inevitably he'll stand and follow you. If, for some illogical reason, he doesn't, at least you'll soon be out of his hearing!

The body language technique in all of this is synchrony. You start the procedure you wish the other person to follow, and the chances are very good that he'll imitate you and complete the action.

I got on a city bus the other day to go downtown, and there were only two other people on it. They were sitting at opposite ends of the bus. The seats ran along either side, and I noticed that as other people got on they always left an empty seat between themselves and the next person. Eventually everyone was spaced one seat apart, and only then did people take the other seats. What's the reason for this?

All of us have certain spatial requirements. Some people in other parts of the world enjoy being very close to each other. In those places, the bus would have filled up with people choosing seats next to each other until there were no empty places. In the United States, most people are uncomfortable when someone comes too close—unless that someone is a close friend.

When there are enough available seats, we usually pick one with an empty seat on either side. When we enter a movie theater that is a part empty, we choose a seat at least three or four seats away from someone else. When we stand in line, if there is available space, we allow a couple of feet between us and the person ahead.

To do otherwise on a bus, in a theater, or on a line is to make a very definite body language statement: "I like you. I am attracted to you. I want to know you better for one reason or another. Therefore I'll ignore the rules and sit right beside you."

We put the rules into words with the old cliché, "A man is entitled to his privacy." His privacy is that extra seat between him and the next person—if it is possible. As long as there are enough vacant seats on a bus, we keep this spacing, and we look askance at the person who violates it by sitting in the seat right next to us.

However, once the bus or theater fills up, someone sitting next to us is no bother at all. We give up our notion of personal space and even return the interloper's apologetic smile.

There are animals, too, who have this same need for personal space and privacy. Watch the way birds position themselves on a wire—they are noncontact animals. Other animals—the walrus for example—is a contact animal. It's happiest when its body is in contact with another walrus. As a rule, man is a noncontact animal, although there are many times when body contact can be a source of comfort and security.

I live in the suburbs, and our neighborhood is mixed, about three-quarters white and one-quarter black. In fact, we have a black family next door. I like Bill, the husband, and I think he likes me. We have a lot in common, and we both try pretty hard to get along. But whenever we have a conversation, I come away with the feeling that Bill just isn't listening to me. Someone suggested that our body language may be different, and I wonder if this could be true.

This could be and usually is true. There are subtle differences in eye contact, looking time, and spatial requirements between blacks and whites. At Boston University, two psychologists, Marianne La France and Clara Mayo, used a hidden camera to film conversations between blacks and whites in order to discover these differences.

One of the basic differences, they found, is that when whites are talking they tend to look away from the other person about half the time. When they're listening, they look at him for much longer, about 85 percent of the time.

Blacks, however, have a completely different pattern of eye contact. They tend to look at someone much more when they're talking.

The Boston psychologists warn that these differences, simple as they seem, can lead to uncomfortable difficulties in communication without either black or white being aware of it.

As an example, they note that when two people are talking and one pauses and looks at his companion, the listener, if he's white, takes this as a signal to begin talking himself. But in a black-white conversation, this wouldn't necessarily signal, "Your turn. I'm finished." Both black and white could end up talking at once.

In turn, the white is used to signaling "your turn" by meeting his companion's eyes. It might not work in a black-white conversation, and there could be an awkward silence while both figured out whose turn it was.

Drs. La France and May also point out that when two whites talk, one looks at the speaker to signal attention. Blacks do not look while listening—again a communication breakdown can take place. The white may feel the black isn't listening, and the black may feel the white is staring at him too much. The result is the uncomfortable feeling you get when you're talking to your neighbor Bill.

Another cause of racial misunderstanding can be due to differences in spatial needs. Dr. Patrick Connolly, of the department of speech and dramatic art at the University of Iowa, studied the different spatial needs of blacks and whites.

Using twenty-four blacks and twenty-four whites, all from eighteen to thirty-three years of age, Connolly showed each pictures of men facing each other at distances varying from twelve to eighty-four inches. Some were pictures of pairs of the same race, and some were mixed.

The viewers were all told that the pictures showed a teacher and student talking, and they were asked to select one picture with the most appropriate spacing for conversation, one where they were too close, and one where they were too far apart.

Whites, Dr. Connolly found, preferred more space between speakers than blacks did. They were most comfortable between twenty-six and twenty-eight inches. Blacks were most comfortable from twenty-one to twenty-four inches. If the space was more than thirty-six inches, the blacks felt the conversation was over, whereas the whites saw forty-four inches as the limit.

Connolly also found that blacks tended to move around more in conversation.

With all this in mind, you may feel that when neighbor Bill comes close to you he's being aggressive or rude, while he may feel that your backing away to your comfortable distance is also a sign of rudeness.

I share an office with another man and it's an economical arrangement. We get along very well—except for this one childish habit he has. When things get out of hand, as they seem to do very often in his business, he'll clench his fist and actually stamp his feet! It seems to me

**that this kind of aggressive action is very immature
for a grown man. What on earth does it mean?**

It means in an adult just what it means in a child—anger.
What the gesture probably comes from is a ritualized
intention to attack. People all over the world, from widely
different cultures, use this gesture as a means of discharging aggression.

If we were to trace it back to animal behavior, we would
find that many male hoofed animals paw the ground
before charging another male. If we favor the theory of
inherited body language, we would say early man had this
same tendency to stamp in his genetic makeup. If we favor
the culturally learned theory of body language, we would
assume that man copied these animal pawings when he
wanted to express aggression.

Whichever is true, we know that men in primitive cultures have, over the centuries, turned their threatening
displays into ritual dances. In the Indian dances of the
Southwest, the angry stamping has turned into a measured
toe-heel step.

With no knowledge of the anthropological background
of the "foot stamp," modern man still is able to dredge the
stamping gesture out of his unconscious and use it when
he grows angry. It seems to be a genuine release of aggression or hostility. That it should be released in just this way
is curious, but not inexplicable. Many bits of human behavior point to an ancient heritage, sometimes going back
to our primate ancestors. We defend our own territory,

and we try to keep a zone of privacy about us as the apes and monkeys do. We like to hold hands with people we love, and so do chimpanzees. We, like the chimps, also, greet each other with kisses.

Somehow, in some way, all these animal gestures have become part of a learned heritage of body language signals—or they have been programmed into our genes. And it is the same way with stamping the foot in anger.

My department in the plant where I work has always been a man's section. Now, with all the flack we've been getting about women's rights, we're beginning to hire women. My problem is that often the things we men think nothing of doing or saying seem to upset the women. Sometimes they don't tell us but let it all stew inside until they blow up. All this is bad for morale, and I wonder, Is there some way of watching their body language to see if they're upset so we men will know when we're wrong?

Two recent scientific studies might be of help to you. One of them, done under a grant from the National Institutes of Mental Health, was designed to find out whether men or women were better at sending body language signals. The researchers showed different pictures to both men and women and let other observers watch them from hidden television circuits. Some of the pictures were pleasant, and some were disturbing. The idea was to see whose expressions the hidden watchers could read most easily, the men or the women.

It turned out that women were better "senders" of body language than men. With these results in mind, the next study from Kansas State University by Anthony and Julie Jurich also questioned a group of people, with hidden television cameras taking it all in. There were only women in this group, and, instead of being shown pictures, they were questioned about very private sexual matters that were bound to make them anxious.

They were asked about kissing, premarital petting, intercourse, and oral-genital sex. Most of the women became increasingly anxious during the interviews, and the hidden cameras caught their body language and relayed it to the researchers to be analyzed.

What did they find out about the body language of women under the stress of anxiety?

For one thing, one classic body language sign of anxiety that researchers used to look for when women were under stress was not obvious in this group. That was the gesture of touching the head along with confusion in speech.

These women showed their anxiety in more subtle ways. Their posture became more rigid than usual, and they avoided eye contact and shifted around uncomfortably. Most of them tried to hide their anxiety.

It seems that your situation in the plant is comparable to this research one. Because they work with men, the women would tend to cover up their anxiety, but the use of "male-centered" speech and action would upset them as the interviews did.

You and the other concerned men should watch for the "uneasiness" that comes when someone avoids eye contact. Nervous people will clear their throats often and use filled pauses excessively—such as "I mean" and "you know" —to avoid hesitation.

Nervousness, a side effect of anxiety, is betrayed by tapping feet and fingers or excessive smoking. The total picture sends a message, and since women are better "senders" than men, you should have little trouble understanding it.

We had a company meeting recently and I presented a proposal. One of the bosses was all for it, but another disapproved. Afterward, I wondered if I could have been more aggressive through the use of body language and whether that would have helped my presentation. I also noticed that I had trouble keeping eye contact with the boss who disapproved.

A speaker usually comes across more aggressively if his body language expresses confidence. A confident, assured man uses his hands comfortably to emphasize his words when he talks. He stands erect, suggesting assurance, and he avoids touching his face, covering his mouth, scratching his head, or rubbing his nose—all gestures that betray uncertainty.

If he's sitting at a desk, a man very certain of his facts

may "steeple" his fingers—join them together and point them upward. This, however, is a gesture that projects a bit of smugness in addition to conviction.

These are all the physical attributes of a strong position when you are presenting ideas. But the strongest position comes from certainty in your own presentation. If you are convinced that it is correct, your conviction will show through in your unconscious body language.

If this conviction is what you describe as aggressive, then your answer is to be sure you believe in your presentation. If you are talking about an aggressive personality, then no amount of body language alone will give it to you. You must change from within and let your outer behavior reflect that change.

You mention some question about eye contact, and this is an important key to approval and disapproval between people. Research at the University of California in Riverside by Dr. Stephen S. Fugito attempted to check out the generally accepted rule that when a person expects approval from someone (as you did from the bosses when you gave your proposal) he increases his eye contact with that person.

Dr. Fugito set up a number of interviews between students and approving and disapproving interviewers of higher and lower status.

He found out that when you talk to someone, executive or fellow worker, you tend to look at him more, make eye contact more often, if he approves than if he disapproves. When you talk to someone who disapproves, you look at him less often, but the duration of each glance stays the same. But when you look at someone who approves of you, the duration of each glance, the moral looking time, increases throughout the conversation.

I went to an office party recently, and I was introduced to one of our foreign salesmen. Instead of just shaking my hand, as we do here in the States, he made a very deep bow. I rather liked it, and I've been wondering, Is there any body language significance to the bow? Where does it come from?

Like many other body language gestures, the bow seems to have come down to us from our primate ancestors. We can see bowing in our close cousins, the chimpanzees. When one chimp invites another to groom him, he makes a deep bow and takes the opposite of a threatening position. This disarms his companion who can then approach him for a grooming session. The bow, in these animals, is a device to turn off aggression.

Primitive humans also used the bow as a gesture of submission. Certainly, when you're bowing you're not able to be aggressive. In those days, rulers demanded the most debasing kind of bows to insure themselves of their subjects' complete obedience. Even in modern times, little more than a hundred years ago among the African people, there were kings who demanded that their subjects throw themselves on the ground some distance away, drag themselves close, and kiss the earth in front of the king.

This is the far end of the scale of self-submission. At the near end, a simple nod acknowledges someone else's presence. In all cases, the gesture reduces your size and makes you less threatening.

Again from the animal world, there is another possible derivation of the bow, farfetched but intriguing. Male monkeys mount the females from behind, and the females bow forward and "submit" to the aggressive mounting. When a male monkey wants to submit to another male, he presents his rear just as the female does.

The aggresive male "mounts" the submissive one, makes a few symbolic "thrusts" without penetrating, and then both go about their business. But from then on the aggressive male is above the other in status. The presentation of the submissive male's buttocks says, "You're stronger than I am and superior."

The whole charade—for that's what it is—has no relationship to animal homosexuality. It's simply a symbolic way of establishing dominance.

Among humans, the African Fulah women, when they greeted a superior, would bow, but bow *away* from him, presenting their buttocks as the primates do. Is it related to the primate "bow," or does it say, in body language, "I am too humble to make eye contact"?

Lest we think this submissive signal is only African, in Europe old fortresses and city gateways from the Middle Ages often have bared buttocks carved on them. Was this to show the threatening invaders the city was submissive, or was it a sign of aggression? The two are often mixed up in the "presentations" of animals. Some monkeys not only submit by presenting their buttocks but also threaten this way, too. In our own college societies, "mooning," presenting the bare buttocks, is a form of contempt, not submission.

I'm the personnel director in a factory, and I am always looking for some way of finding independent people during my personnel interviews. Not that I feel there is anything wrong with a dependent person in a work situation, but I do feel that some of our jobs are perfect for people with aggressive, independent attitudes, while others are just right for more passive workers. Could I discover the independent ones by using my own body language, or is there some way I could read theirs?

First, let's consider the body language of the man being interviewed. Unfortunately, there are no reliable body language clues that would definitely identify independence as a personality trait. You tend to confuse aggression and independence. True, an independent person is often aggressive, but sometimes he isn't—just as some aggressive people are dependent.

Some observers have tentatively linked aggression to good posture, by which they mean an erect, self-confident stance, and to an "open, alert face," but these are just overall impressions, and anyone can fake them, even dependent people.

An attempt to be more scientific about identifying

independent people was made at the University of North Dakota by Michael J. Galton and John D. Tyler. Reporting in the *Journal of Social Psychology*, the two men suggested that "dependent people, because of their excessive reliance on others for approval" might be unusally sensitive to other people's body language.

Using psychological examinations, they tested students to discover just how dependent or independent they were. While this can't be done by watching body language, it can be done with written tests. They selected twenty-four students, twelve who were classfied as dependent and twelve classified as independent. Then a series of six minute interviews were conducted with these students.

The questions asked were all "non threatening," calculated not to excite the students, but the body language of the questioner was a different matter. For the first three minutes of the interview, he would use a *positive* body language. He would face the student, lean forward, maintain eye contact, and smile often. Then he would switch, and for the next three minutes he would use *negative* body language. He would lean back in his chair, turn away from the student, avoid eye contact, and stop smiling.

The interviews were recorded on videotape by hidden cameras and then analyzed carefully, Unfortunately, all that the researchers could find out was was that all the students interviewed reacted positively to *positive* body language and negatively to *negative* body language. It didn't matter whether they were independent or dependent; they all reacted the same way.

The experiment failed, but in failing proved that you get more out of people with positive body language. For you, as a personnel director, I can only suggest that you forget body language as an attempt to classify your workers. You might, however, try some of the written personality tests.

My little girl Annie is aggressive and outgoing with other children, but I've noticed that when she plays alone she laughs a lot less. I wonder why this is and whether grown-ups also laugh more when they're with other people.

It's logical that all of us, adults and children, would laugh more often when we're with someone else. When we're alone we would have to remember, read, or see something funny in order to laugh. But in interaction with another person there are many possibilities that can lead to laughter. The fact that Annie is aggressive means that she is more easily stimulated by other children simply because she is able to meet them without shyness.

What is intriguing about our laughter when we are with someone else is its relationship to humor. Do we find things funny when we are alone as often as when we are with others? Or, put differently, what impression does the laughter of others have on us? Do we laugh more when we see others laugh? Do things seem funnier to us when someone else laughs at them, or, for that matter, do ordinary things seem funny when someone else laughs at them?

In an attempt to discover the effect of other children's laughter on a child exposed to humor, a couple of researchers from the Wales Institute of Science and Technology had groups of seven- and eight-year-old children listen to humorous material with nine-year-old friends. The nine-year-olds were given secret instructions to laugh at certain things, funny and unfunny.

The researchers found that when the nine-year-olds laughed, the younger children laughed and smiled more and thought the material they listened to funnier than it really was.

Any of us who watch sit-com shows on television could have predicted these findings. Certainly the television producers are well aware of them, and by using canned laughter on the programs they hope to condition us to laugh at what they consider funny—not what our independent thinking tells us is funny.

The potential in this nonverbal programming is frightening. If we can be programmed to think inanities are funny, then surely this behavior modification can be applied to other areas beside laughter. We can be programmed to hate, if hate is made desirable, to accept violence—how many western and police programs does it take to desensitize us to murder and mayhem; and, on an even more troubling note, we can surely be programmed to accept and vote for the political figure of the programmer's choice!

I am the business manager for a firm that recently took over two floors of a new building. I have to help design the various offices, but we don't have enough space to give private offices to everyone. Already, some people are very aggressive in their complaints about being cramped. Are there any hints in body language that would help me work this out?

Body language includes the way we handle space, and an understanding of this can help you in your problem. I once shared an office with another man, a small room, and we both felt cramped and unhappy and spent half our time complaining about the arrangement.

Then, one inspired day, we rearranged the desks so that neither of us touched a wall when we reached out. It changed our entire mood. We no longer felt hemmed in.

Progressive management must become aware of man's need for space and how he handles space. They must also know just how much space a man requires if he is to feel at ease. A basic rule is the one my friend and I demonstrated. If a man can reach out in every direction without touching a wall, he won't feel cramped.

On the other hand, secretaries in "bullpens" feel open and vulnerable. It's a case of too much space around them. Give them cubicles and they feel better. Raise the cubicle walls to about six feet and they feel private and more secure and they work better. Make the cubicle too small and they feel hemmed in—too large and they're lost.

One of the lessons architects have learned from management's use and misuse of space came from a study on work production at Western Electric Company many years ago. The lesson was called the Hawthorne effect, and it stated that production rises as working conditions improve.

Further study of the Hawthorne effect pared it down to stimulation from the environment as well as a radical change in attitude on the part of personnel.

Stimulation from the environment is one clue to how you can manage the space needs of the men who work for your company. This stimulus has been interpreted by architects and designers in various ways, from a pleasing use of color to plants, lights, music, and a change in interpersonnel relationships. In one office, production increased when management became more accessible to the workers.

A second key is privacy, but in the United States privacy is generally linked to visual protection. Glass cubicles and doors are disliked by the workers. Frosted glass is a step above, and of course a closed office is most desirable.

In France, by contrast, the supervisor is usually positioned out in the open in plain view of the workers to give them confidence and him status.

I've been going with a young man who is blind. We both feel that we're in love, but there is one thing about him that troubles me. When he tells me he's happy his face has an expressionless look. Why isn't he more aggressive about showing his feelings?

"Showing your feelings" is something you learn. While it's true that aggressive people are more apt to reveal themselves—as if to say "This is how I feel. Take me or leave me!"—while passive people will often cover up their true feelings and present the type of face the world wants to see, this rule doesn't always work. Many aggressive people wear a mask and use their aggression to push the type of emotion they want the world to read, even as many passive people are able to face the world with their true emotions showing.

However, in your friend's case, I don't think lack of aggression has anything to do with it. Like the rest of body language, facial expression is hooked to culture and learned in much the same way that we learn our native language—by imitation.

A blind person (if he's been blind from birth) has no opportunity to imitate, for other people's faces are closed books. If a person loses his sight after he has learned body language, he has had a chance to learn facial expressions, too. For this reason, people born blind tend to look flat and expressionless without showing what they really feel.

Some gestures, interestingly enough, are used by blind people even when they've never had a chance to learn them. Behaviorist Irenaus Eibel-Eibesfeldt reports that he has observed a small boy, born blind, hiding his face in embarrassment. Obviously this gesture couldn't have been learned, but is it truly genetic, handed down from primitive man, and even beyond, from the animals? Certainly people all over the world hide their faces when they are embarrassed. How did the little blind boy learn to do this?

This is an area in body language still relatively unexplored, but fascinating.

I am a normally mild person, and I find that I'm very disturbed by all the aggression that I find around me. People at work, in my family, and even strangers in the street seem "out to get you" all the time. I've been very seriously thinking of trying to find some simpler, more easygoing society and moving there. Does the body language of other societies indicate that any of them have no aggression?

It would be hard to find a society without agression. Scientists aren't in complete agreement about agression in human behavior. It may be that every culture has some, though certainly there is less in some societies—or at least outwardly there is less.

Eskimos are generally considered without aggression because they never developed the concept of warfare, village against village or tribe against tribe. But they will show aggression within their own tribe or family. People who have studied Eskimo culture report that it is not uncommon for an Eskimo to beat his wife or fight with another man, but this kind of aggression, the kind you object to, may be a natural attribute of the human condition. Certainly, no anthropologist has described a society free of aggression.

As for one culture being more aggressive than another, that, too, is questionable. *Threat display,* a means of aggression existing in animals and primitive societies where men use ornaments to make themselves frightening to their enemies, also exists in one form or another in our society. Men try to make themselves look taller (even wearing high heels) and broader (jackets with padded shoulders) to impress and dominate others.

Culturally, we all, in every society, accept courage as a virtue. Even pacifists try to be courageous in demonstrating for peace. The intellect may abhor aggression, but the emotion appreciates it.

Humans find a great deal of pleasure in aggression, no matter how "civilized" they are. Our sports are all based on aggression, and the worldwide Olympic games are the ultimate in controlled aggression.

A very good case has been made for the necessity of aggression, or at least for this type of controlled aggression. It discharges the aggressive impulses that everyone seems to have.

An interesting experiment was reported in the *Journal of Abnormal Social Psychology* by Drs. J. E. Hokanson and S. Shetler to show how important discharging aggression is to human beings. A group of students were intentionally annoyed, and their blood pressure rose drastically. They were then told that the man who had annoyed them would now have to solve some problems under their guidance. Half the men were told that if he made an error, they could signal it to him with an electric shock. The other half could only activate a light for him to see.

The blood pressure of the group who believed they were shocking the man who had annoyed them dropped to normal rapidly. The pressure of the men who could only flash a light remained high!

This experiment tells us how necessary it is for humans to get rid of their aggressive impulses and also how wrong it would be to live in a society where no aggression occurred. Bottled up, aggression could destroy us. When it is released, we are able to survive.

The best you could hope to find is some society where some ritualized form of release from aggression allowed the people to blow their safety valves when necessary. The release needn't be aggression in an ugly sense against our neighbors, family, or friends. It can be competetive aggression in business, politics, or sports, or creative aggression in the arts, in painting, sculpture, building—in almost any field of endeavor. Even in communist countries where a lot of noise is made about nonaggression, safety valves occur in aggression against other countries, against dissidents, and in cultural revolutions and five-year plans.

Channeled aggression, useful aggression, can improve a society. The form your question should take, the form in which an answer would help you most, is, What area in society can I find where my own bottled-up aggression can be usefully released?